MANY PATROLS

REMINISCENCES OF A GAME OFFICER

R.D. Symons
1898 - 1973

MANY PATROLS

REMINISCENCES OF A GAME OFFICER

R.D. SYMONS

COTEAU BOOKS

Edited by Dave Margoshes.
Cover photograph of R.D. Symons, courtesy of Marygold Globeil.
Cover design by Next Communications.
Book design and typesetting by Val Jakubowski.
Printed and bound in Canada.

The publisher gratefully acknowledges the financial assistance of the Saskatchewan Arts Board, the Canada Council, the Department of Canadian Heritage, and the City of Regina Arts Commission.

All line drawings are by R.D. Symons and are housed in the R.D. Symons Collection of the Saskatchewan Archives Board. The frontispiece photograph of Symons is from the same collection. Permission to reproduce the illustrations and photograph have been granted by Marygold Globeil.

Map details are taken from the 1939 Highway Map of Saskatchewan (Map B452), courtesy of the Saskatchewan Archives Board.

Canadian Cataloguing in Publication Data

Symons, R. D. (Robert David), 1898-1973

    Many patrols

    ISBN 1-55050-073-2

1. Symons, R. D. (Robert David), 1898-1973.
2. Game wardens - Saskatchewan - Biography.
3. Wildlife conservation - Saskatchewan. I. Title.

SK354.S95A3 1994   639.9'092   C94 -920172-3

COTEAU BOOKS
401-2206 Dewdney Ave
Regina, SK   S4R 1H3

"Idlers, game preservers, and mere human clotheshorses"
— Carlyle

"Gained universal applause by explaining a passage of the Game Act"
— Sir Richard Steele

CONTENTS

INTRODUCTION

I FIRST HEARD OF the writer and artist Robert David Symons when a visiting writer/naturalist sang his praises. The name was familiar to me; I think I had heard him mentioned by local people as someone who had understood nature close to home and in the way in which they did themselves: that is, more from daily observation than in a specialized, scientific way, and also with a certain reverence devoid, though, of sentimentality, although I did not know that at the time. I had dismissed Symons without even looking him up, thinking his books most likely homespun, shallow and self-congratulatory volumes about a country life. But when the young man, who had a university education in the sciences, praised them, I capitulated, and went to the small library in Eastend, intending to order them, only to find his books so popular that *Silton Seasons* was sitting there on the shelf. So, belatedly, like a good many before me, I discovered a Saskatchewan original.

Many Patrols: Reminiscences of a Game Officer is the story of the fifteen years (beginning in 1926) that Symons spent in Saskatchewan, mostly in the Battlefords area, but also in the northeast and finally in the Cypress Hills district, as a "peace officer" or "game guardian," the forerunner of today's conservation officers. We see Symons as he gradually goes beyond mere law enforcement to a wider understanding of the necessity of protecting the natural environment, till he eventually arrives at the sensibility of today's environmentalists – fully developed but fifty years ahead of them.

Although he doesn't appear to have seen himself in that light, Symons may also be viewed as a pioneer, having arrived in Saskatchewan from England in 1914 at the age of sixteen. Whether he was always a lover of nature or became one when he first saw Saskatchewan, we do not know, but it appears he fitted himself to the countryside as it was as soon as he saw it, a feat which took most immigrants a full lifetime and often into the next generation to accomplish. In time, Symons came to know the wilds of Saskatchewan better than most of us born here.

As a game guardian, he was courageous and resourceful, taking his work with seriousness and accepting his responsibility to a degree few would do today. There is something of the noble English hero, the White Knight, of Sir Galahad or Horatio Nelson in Robert David Symons – a little incongruous, a little anachronistic in the humble bush country of Saskatchewan. Nonetheless, he succeeds in snaring the reader in his view. We might wish to dislike Symons for this, but the code is an admirable one that served the British and their empire well for a very long time, and Symons, straight as a die, as they say, fully embodied that honourable standard.

Yet the southern half of the province was already a settled place when he saw it. Only the forests of the northeast were still wild enough that in at least one area he broke the first trail. He first knew First Nations peoples when they had already been confined to reserves but before they had accepted all the trappings of the Europeans' way of life, and he expresses his admiration for them. He also knew the Metis well and, if there is some condescension in his attitude toward both of them, he was not ignorant of the causes of their present condition, and his sympathy for them appears genuine: he mourns along with them for all that they lost.

He saw, too, the places where, none too honourably, white society – the society of Europeans – touched the lives of the Metis and First Nations peoples; he could make himself welcome in all their homes, where he paid attention and is consequently able to give us a picture of the province of the time, on the edge of the last North American frontier, where the wild and those who would tame it and claim it for their own met in an uneasy line.

This was a harsh time in our history, and the Saskatchewan Symons tells us about was not that of established society, the dinner tables and at-homes of the small frontier mansions of Regina or Prince Albert. It is a picture of life on the margins of that official society – but it is not the clean, warmhearted one of our folklore and family memories. He saw the settlers – the farmers, ranchers and squatters – not as himself a member of their raggle-taggle society, but as an observer who travelled from town to town and farm to farm watching them, learning their habits and their way of life and noting the ragged edges that sometimes needed trimming.

These were a people scrabbling for a living on none-too-forgiving soil, augmenting their incomes with the fish and with deer, moose and elk meat, and with ducks, geese and whatever other edible birds and animals presented themselves, often whether in season or out, often whether it was legal to shoot them or not. Game was plentiful, and there was no shortage of poachers or those who would kill indiscriminately in order to make a living selling the meat. Symons's response to this was to pursue offenders singlemindedly and without favouritism, yet always tempering his prosecution with compassion. He saw much poverty and was never unaffected by it; he sometimes paid offenders' fines out of his own pocket. His work required infinite patience, a clear, even a cunning mind, and courage, since on occasion his life was in danger, which, rather than intimidating him, appeared to increase his zest for his work.

His literary style and his command of self, his sympathy for and his intense love of this planet, reminded me at once of the many books which I admire, and which greatly influenced me, by Laurens van der Post. These are books about specific wildernesses and the people and animals within them and the ways in which sojourns in these faraway and difficult places might remind one of the travails and triumphs of the human spirit in its universality, whether in Africa, England or the bush and lake country of central Saskatchewan.

Many Patrols and other books by Symons sound another echo: it is the echo of the work of the much-revered American conservationist, Aldo Leopold (1887-1948), author of *A Sand County Almanac,* published the year after his death and since become a classic of environmental literature. Although Leopold was a near contemporary of Symons, and rapidly became a saint of today's conservationist movement, Symons, while offering much the same message, was relatively unknown, particularly among the new generation of urban environmentalists, despite his popularity – in the U.S. as well as Canada – during the seventies as a nostalgasizer of the simpler lifestyle of the vanishing rural West. Part of this can be attributed to Symons's lowly position as a rank-and-file employee of the provincial government – a game guardian! – but it is also because his first books weren't published until the mid-sixties, by which time Leopold had already been dead for fifteen years and, having initiated the first Forest Wilderness area in the United States and become a founder of the Wilderness Society, was in the front ranks of North American conservationists.

Symons published eight books, including an historical novel about Saskatchewan. In the current climate of heightened interest in works by Saskatchewan authors, and the rising interest generally in works about nature which accompanies the environmental movement, the publication of *Many Patrols*, one of his earliest writing efforts but, ironically, the last to be published – more than twenty years after his death – will alert readers to the existence of his earlier books, will perhaps bring them back into print, and thus at last give to him the place in our province's literary canon, and indeed, its history, which he has for so long deserved.

SHARON BUTALA
EASTEND, SASKATCHEWAN

PREFACE

IN THE FOLLOWING PAGES I hope my readers may obtain a glimpse into the activities of a game guardian in the 1920s and 1930s, as well as into the struggle to foster the continuance of the wonderful wildlife of Western Canada, a struggle the outcome of which was to exceed our fondest expectations within less than twenty years. If much of the advantage so gained has subsequently been lost, this can only be explained by the abandonment of our field, in line with changing concepts, to technological methods which are at once inelastic and based on the unnatural premise that, with "modern" education, human nature itself changes – which it emphatically does *not*.

In spite of claims of the educators and the sociologists, riches do not breed unselfishness, nor does college training banish for ever sin and crime, so the enforcement arm should not be lifted to please these theorists. As well say we can educate people not to rob banks, and so fire the police force.

Certainly we cannot expect the ordinary policeman – with all his rectitude and his training – to handle the ordinances especially applying to game and wildlife, where dedication is required to a *cause* as well as to the *law*.

The institution of law officers is not new and will never be old. The three arms of the law are equally necessary and equally to be respected. Members of the RCMP and the various provincial, city and town police forces, together with such specialized or subsidiary forces as game and fishery officers, rangers and traffic or highway officers, form that third arm of the law which acts in liaison with the legislators and the courts which ultimately enforce it.

The work of the peace officer is an honourable activity, in spite of those who may not live up to its true interpretation and in spite of the disrepute in which much work is sometimes held by a public which has not always been prepared to try to understand it.

I am afraid that, for the sake of truth, I shall have to admit that disrespect of the law is far too common in Western Canada. The rule of law is not fully understood. I say this as an ex-peace officer and as a resident of the West since my youth. So I hope no feelings will be hurt and no offence taken when I say there *is* room for criticism, which might better come kindly from within than unkindly from without our borders.

My personal reasons for becoming a game officer were based on a very earnest desire to help in preserving wildlife in the best way I knew – by giving it real protection. I still think that is the way. I am not by nature one who cares to pry into other people's affairs. Naturally I look back with a certain satisfaction on my work, but that satisfaction is not based on any pleasure derived from prosecuting my fellows and seeing them convicted and fined. The pleasure was in knowing that sportsmen – *real* sportsman – were able to have their share of hunting, while the wild things, not being taken advantage of, were still able to maintain, if not increase, their numbers. Conviction of offenders was a necessary means to this end.

When I took the oath to do my duty "without fear or favour," I knew that "without fear" did not mean that I should not take necessary precautions to guard my own safety. I equally realized that "without favour" did not mean without compassion, mercy or understanding, or without very careful consideration of all and every extenuating circumstance. It is no small thing to put in jeopardy a man's good name, his worldly goods or his freedom. One had often, however, to harden one's heart for the sake of that greater and more all-embracing freedom which only the Rule of Law can maintain. If the hunter must be free to follow his sport, that gives him no right to deprive the naturalist or the nature lover of *his* freedom to see and observe the wildlife of his choice.

NOTE: Throughout this book, I have concealed names and places whenever I thought there might be cause for embarrassment, and for the same reason I have waited for many years to compile it. The incidents are otherwise completely true.

I

A LIFE IN THE BUSH

I BECAME A GAME guardian in 1926. I'd been ranching in the Arm River country west of Regina, and had an appointment as a voluntary guardian, but in 1926 I was forced to close down my ranch due to dwindling grazing lands. I was casting about for my next step when, out of the blue, I received a letter from Chief Game Guardian Fred Bradshaw asking if I'd like to be part of his slowly growing staff. I agreed and promptly joined, never dreaming this would be my occupation for the next fifteen years.

I had first met Mr. Bradshaw in 1916 when I was a lad of eighteen, only two years in the country and training in the Canadian Army in preparation for a return trip overseas. My regiment was housed in the old Winter Fair Building which stood on the then bald-headed prairie near the Mounted Police barracks on the west side of Regina.

I saw by a brief notice in the paper that a Mr. Bradshaw of the Department of Agriculture would be giving a lecture on prairie birds at the City Hall that week. Always interested in natural history, I attended, and enjoyed the talk immensely. Mr. Bradshaw made an earnest plea for conservation, and showed many lantern slides of common birds such as meadowlarks and blackbirds. I had the courage to introduce myself to him after the lecture, and thus began a long friendship. On my return from overseas, I kept in correspondence with him. He was at that time engaged in forming a nucleus from which emerged the Museum of Natural History (now the Royal Saskatchewan Museum) in Regina.

When Europeans had come to what is now the province of Saskatchewan, it was a land teeming with game.

The prairies offered cover and feed to countless bison and great herds of antelope and elk, as well as to grouse, crane and other birds. Above all, thousands of shining lakes and millions of small potholes and sloughs harboured ducks, geese and other waterfowl in hordes which darkened the skies.

Even as early as the 1800s, it was recognized that measures would have to be taken if this great natural resource was not to vanish.

The North West Game Act called for some licencing regulations, and set certain basic closed seasons, but it was both loosely worded and loosely enforced. On the whole, that act never became well known, and at any rate it was looked upon with disfavour by the hardy frontiersmen of the day.

However, it did set a rough pattern as well as a precedent for the later Game Act of Saskatchewan when it was enacted shortly after the formation of that province in 1905.

For the first ten years, this act, like its predecessor, was hardly observed, this time due to the fact that settlers were pouring in to the West from both Europe and the United States. The early Americans certainly never did have much regard for what they considered were restraining and liberty-threatening laws, while the European peasant, hardly able to understand English, simply never heard of them.

Hardly had the dust from the newcomers' wagons settled when war was declared in Europe in 1914. The police forces were trimmed to the bone to fill the marching ranks, and the cry was to produce. All else was lost sight of in this great war effort, and the termination of the conflict found our wildlife in the greatest jeopardy. The prairies were settled, and the few surviving antelope and sage hens were confined to the more arid areas of grazing land still left to the ranchers. In the north, settlers were also beginning to penetrate and the lumber industry was cutting a wide swath, supplying its camps mainly with wild game.

Many earlier settlers augmented the income from their meager crops with the dollars they could earn from trapping beaver, muskrat and weasel, while hounds for hunting coyotes were found on more and more of the farms and ranches, activities which extended to running any other game they saw, especially deer.

Under the pressure of supplying not only the native Indians, but also the farmers, lumbermen and survey and exploring parties, it is small wonder that many people thought our wildlife was inevitably doomed, and some even cared not, for, said they, "These creatures have fulfilled their purpose, and what further need have we of them?"

There were others who thought differently, who thought there was still a chance, myself among them. One in particular, however, was Fred Bradshaw, who had come from England to work with the new Department of Agriculture. For me, it was to be a great honour to work with him and to contribute to what I considered then – and still do – a highly worthy cause.

In order to pursue my duties, I was armed with a cheap metal badge, a constable's manual, copies of both the Game Act and the Migratory Birds Act and reams of forms and paper for preparing the endless reports I would soon come to be familiar with, although Mr. Bradshaw made it clear to me that "reports can always wait, but the job cannot." My patrols, he told me, were the important thing.

The chief game guardian cautioned me, too, that I would have to feel my way and use my head. "Never forget that you are backed by the full power of the law," he told me, "so you need have no fear. At the same time, you must be careful never to abuse your power." The first consideration, Mr. Bradshaw counselled, must be the prevention of crime, meaning that in many cases a few words of warning would have as good an effect as prosecution. "We must never persecute," he said, "for that will defeat our purposes."

With these stirring words ringing in my ears, I set out for my headquarters at Battleford, the early seat of the territorial government, with its Land Office, Court House and Indian Agency, before the development of the brash young city just across the swift North Saskatchewan River. My pay was to be one hundred dollars a month, a good sum in those days, though it was reduced to seventy-five dollars after the onset of the Depression in 1929 and was not restored to its old level until 1932 or 1933, and never exceeded one hundred and twenty-five dollars during my fifteen-year tenure. In addition, I was entitled to an allowance of five cents per mile for the use for a saddle horse. I mentally calculated how many nickels it would take to pay for Billy (the big bay) and Chief (the buckskin), which I had already purchased for two hundred dollars each, plus their shoeing, stabling and fodder.

For patrols on foot there was no allowance. A man was evidently worth less than a horse! Boat hire, when needed, would be paid for at fifty cents a day. When in the settled country, meals at thirty-five cents and lodging at one dollar was allowed, but under no circumstances would the department approve expenses in excess of seventy-five dollars per month. Payment for a car, if I ever used one, would be at ten cents per mile. There was no allowance for sleeping on the prairie or camping in the bush. Patrol sheets, monthly diaries, pens, ink and paper could be requisitioned on the forms provided.

Battleford might well have been singled out as expressing for the whole province that feeling of live-and-let-live, help-your-neighbour spirit which prevented those hungry years from working altogether for evil, a spirit which has finally brought about so much good work in the alleviation of poverty and hopelessness; and, if some of us, including myself, feel that socialism went too far and that the welfare state may perhaps present an evil face at times, this is not to belittle those who gave their goods and their time to hasten it.

The spirit of Battleford had been forged in troublous times. This town had been the seat of the first government of the North West, a country of many Metis and more Indians, proud in their poverty, wise in their simplicity, representing a day whose sun has set.

There were traders – French and English – who foresaw a great city, only to be finally disappointed when the railway passed north of the river, instead of across the beautiful scenic plain sheltered on the north by the banks of the Saskatchewan and on the south by the hazy blue ridge of the Eagle Hills.

The Riel Rebellion had not been kind to Battleford. Ugly whispers had arisen of a threatened Cree attack – whispers which may well have been born of wishful thinking on the part of some who sought military glory. The result of the near-conflict further embarrassed those once proud hunters of the buffalo, so that more and more the Church must be their mother and the Indian Agent their father.

Forged in the furnace of different religions, races and ideologies, the spirit of Battleford emerged a little crooked, far from perfect, but still the best thing of its kind; for it was hammered out by men of good will, men of purpose, men free – or as free as those days allowed – from the petty racialism which then characterized so much of the civilized world.

I first met old Chief Fine Day, who had been a war leader in the days of Poundmaker, in the roomy general store which dealt in everything from axes to sugar, and had been founded by the Prince family from what was called "way back."

Thereafter (I had picked up enough Cree for practical purposes), many were the good hours I spent with him, sitting before his tent on the Sweetgrass Reserve, sometimes joined by Chief Sam Swimmer, with the smoke curling from the inverted wash-tub now used as a cooking stove, and the old chief smoking without embarrassment the tobacco I had brought him. His eyes would look to the *O'Saskatchewanik*, the Sliding Hill of *Wīsahkecāhk*, and he would tell me of running buffalo on the plains, or, pulling aside his thin blanket, show me the ugly scars on his arm and tell me of the grizzly bear which almost took his life on the cliffs of the Cypress Hills in the days when he and his people were free and the plough of the white man had not swallowed up the Garden of the Manito.

The Indians came to Battleford from miles around, and they never had a better friend than Paul Prince, whose father, the old senator, had not only built a store, but a tradition which lived on in spite of the shiny new chain markets in the "North Town." During those desperately hard years of the thirties, I know of no man, white, Metis or Indian, whose family ever really wanted for the necessities while that sign "B. Prince & Sons" faced the main street of Battleford. One can only guess at the extent of the unpaid bills which gradually accumulated, but Paul was a man who held simply to the faith in which he had been reared, a faith which taught the blessings of giving. If his natural concern for the welfare of his own family may have shortened his life, that is how he would have wished it.

There were others, too, perhaps of a different belief, but equally faithful to the common precepts. There were pagan Indians whose word was better than many a man's bond. There was Tommy Turnham, the butcher – only the angel with the book and pen could tell you how often he turned his back when Indian women came to the slaughterhouse for offal and took something better which might fill their hungry children with good broth.

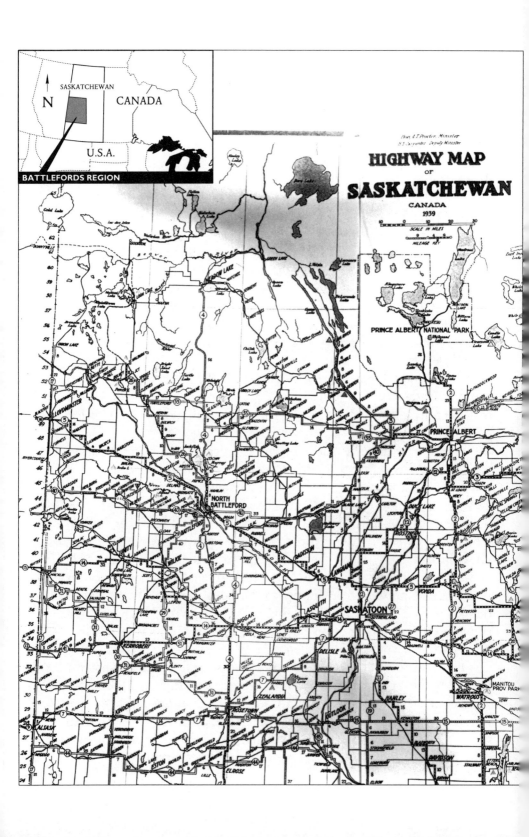

The Indians remained stoical, and accepted their fate with dignity. The bond of the frontier still embanded the alloyed and transmuted metal, and in the remaining government offices the Naults and the Lateurs polished their stools side by side with the Ridingtons, the MacLeays and the Burlinghams. Harry Adams, the *okimāwisis* of the Hudson Bay (by now town clerk), was as English as the Clinskills were Scottish or the Davises Welsh, but all were heir to the traditions of the old Northwest, and French, Cree and English were the tongues they spoke. But one result of the Rebellion, so soon followed by the rush of settlers from Europe and the States, was that the coup de grâce was given to the French language and to biculturalism in the West.

The area I was to patrol was an empire in itself – from the Shell River just west of Prince Albert westward to the Alberta border at Meridian Ferry, Lloydminster and Macklin, and from Biggar and Big Manitou Lake on the south to the Bronson and Meadow Lake forests to the north.

The scenery here is some of the finest in the prairie provinces. South of the North Saskatchewan from Sonningdale westward, lie the wooded heights of the Eagle Hills, broken by many deep and tortuous ravines. To the south and west lie the open plains of Wilkie and Unity, merging into the rolling, lake-gemmed sandhills of Manito Forest Reserve, at that time still under the wing of the Dominion Department of the Interior. Just south of Battleford, lay the Mosquito, Grizzly Bear and Red Pheasant Indian reserves, while eastward along the Battle River the Sweetgrass, Little Pine and Poundmaker reserves were still held by their original owners – or at least by their descendants, for of those who had accepted the treaty in person only a few like Sam Swimmer and Fine Day remained.

Bishop Grandin, Father Lacombe and the great French families who had done so much to help the building of the West in these parts were forgotten; and few of the newcomers, passing rapidly through Eastern Canada on their way to the new El Dorado, knew more about the Indians than that they were a vanished, or vanishing, race which had retreated to the fastness of the northern wilderness.

Northward and westward are the rough area of Big Gully Creek and the precipitous slopes of Pikes Peak, where Kenderdine the artist had his original ranch. Still north, across the river, are Frenchman's Butte (famous from Rebellion days), Horse Hill and the English River. Further east again are the Moon Hills, the Thickwood Hills, the lake country of Marcelin and the rolling beauty of the Mistawasis Indian Reserve. Still further north are the Bronson and Meadow Lake forests, dark and gloomy and then home of moose and bear and other fur-bearing animals.

In those days, the southern part of this area was spotted thickly with sloughs of all sizes, offering both resting and nesting sanctuary for waterfowl, while north of the river lay – as they do now – that chain of wide, placid lakes which then, with the exception of Jackfish and Murray, had not yet seen the summer cottage or heard the power boat. These were all famous for their whitefish and pickerel.

From the prairies in the south to the aspen parklands of Battle River and Maidstone, from the mixed forests and sombre spruce woods of Midnight Lake, Mont Nebo and Bellebutte, to the tangled brule and treacherous muskegs of the Bronson, every aspect pleased, and only the poacher was vile, for woodlands that might have supported thousands of deer held but few. Killing out of season, killing for sale to camps, killing of does and fawns, wastage and greed had done their work.

In the fall, the ducks and geese of the wetlands had little rest, and hunters loved to be photographed in front of long strings of bloody and disheveled wildfowl taken far in excess of either need or sportsman-ship.

The few beaver dams left were annually depleted of their increase by the fur poachers, who knew well how to smuggle their loot to the marketeers in the larger cities, thus evading both the royalty payable to the province and the danger of prosecution. The nearest game guardian had heretofore come from Saskatoon, and his few and hurried patrols had been by the Ford car of that period, which confined him to the few main roads fit for that type of transportation. Poachers operating by horseback, team, boat, or on foot, and, knowing every inch of the country, could easily evade apprehension.

Once in Battleford, I had much to do. I studied everything I could find about law and a peace officer's duty. Among the books I was able to borrow was one (I forget its name and its author) which quoted a famous member of the French Sureté to this effect: "It is essential that a police officer be able to take any insult, any lies, any affronts, without betraying annoyance or personal antagonism. He must not argue, he must not accuse, he must only be concerned with evidence."

However, the writer went on, "The police officer must create an 'atmosphere.' He must be deliberate, he must not argue, he must show that he has the situation in hand, and never let it get out of hand. He must not let his thoughts be distracted by protestations or threats, much less by a confiding manner. He must show himself unbiased by public opinion for or against the accused. This is not to say that a complaint made by an honest member of the public must be disregarded, but rather he must determine if possible whether a complaint is honest or the result of spite."

This "atmosphere" I always strove to create. Even outward appearance helped, so I shaved meticulously, even out in the bush, and I took care that my clothes were tidy, my boots shined, and my horse curried and with clean saddlery. I invariably addressed men as "sir" and women as "madam."

It was sometimes very hard to take the abuse that an accused person would heap on me, but I received an uncommonly good lesson in this matter on an occasion when I attended a police court to study procedure. A young constable was waxing quite indignant, while giving evidence, over the fact that the accused had sworn at him and lied to him. He was interrupted by the magistrate, who struck the desk with his gavel and said, "Constable, the court is not interested in your feelings at this or any other time; after all, what are policemen for except to be sworn at and lied to? Pray continue your evidence."

Next, I made a general patrol to acquaint myself with the area, which meant calling at every town and village. This was chiefly to visit the issuers of game licences, most of whom were rather frigid at the start, and well they might be. I could see them thinking hard and sizing me up. I well knew that some of them were not above hunting themselves without benefit of licence, or, worse, allowing their friends to do so, in spite of the fact that by virtue of their appointments they were themselves honorary game guardians and bound to assist me.

Usually, the issuers were keepers of hardware stores or general merchants, and combined their job with the sale of hunting and fishing supplies. Not a few took furs in general trade. Fur dealers, too, had to have licences, which were the only ones issued directly from Regina, for the reason that they required the submission of an application form and an affidavit, as residents outside the province were required to pay a higher fee.

I was quite aware that several of these licence issuers dealt in furs illegally; but, since it was still summer and no fur was moving, I felt sure that my inquiries about fur dealers generally would act as a hint to all but the boldest. This proved to be correct, for shortly afterwards applications began to dribble in, and by fall twice as many fur dealers were licenced as before.

All furs were subject to a small royalty upon leaving the province, and it was impossible to control these payments unless dealers were licenced, for only known dealers could be obliged to keep records. These records had to show the number and kind of furs purchased, with the trapper's name and licence number. In the case of treaty Indians, who needed no licence, the trapper's treaty number would be shown. Sales and the licence number of the travelling dealer also had to be reported.

My concern, then, was to see that both trappers and fur dealers were licenced, and that the records were properly kept in books supplied by the department. I had to arrest a good many dealers before I could persuade that fraternity we meant what we said.

Furs at this time were fetching a good price, and many people put their finger into the trading pie. Storekeepers took furs on account; travelling cattle buyers picked them up as a sideline; even some missionaries took furs in lieu of contributions.

All this could start a whole chain of operations. The unlicenced trapper would seek an unlicenced fur dealer to sell his catch to; the unlicenced storekeeper would contact an unlicenced travelling dealer, perhaps a cattle buyer; and he, in turn, would put the furs in his suitcase or trunk and take them to a market in Winnipeg or Montreal. From the woods to Milady's coat there would be no record of the various transactions.

Hundreds of thousands of dollars had been lost in past years through evasion of these royalties, but, as we tightened up and became experienced, we stopped the full flood, though there remained an irritating dribble.

The foregoing applied mainly to farming areas, and involved mostly the pelts of coyotes, skunks, badgers and weasels.

On the farm, trapping was an extra source of revenue rather than a full-time occupation, which made it harder to control. In the north, a trapper could not conceal his operations in the same way, and the fur trade was pretty well in the hands of the Hudson's Bay Company, which found it more profitable to conduct its extensive business on orthodox lines with a proper accounting system, and therefore paid its royalty fees without demur or fuss. In any case, the men of the company were not the sort of people who cheat; it is only fair to say that the term "Honourable Company" was not without meaning.

At the time of which I write, the game laws were, in general, based on a few fundamental and important protective policies which had been well understood for years, and which were well known to stockmen and ranchers.

These were, briefly, the protection at all times of female big game and their young, and of males throughout the rut. Therefore, open season on moose, deer and caribou did not start until after the breeding season – that is, until November 15; this made "calling" moose unlawful. Early snow, making good tracking, was often a temptation to hunters in October and early November. This called for vigilance on the part of game officers, as did the running of big game with hounds, with a resultant loss of females and young.

The protection of game birds was on the same basis. Spring shooting of ducks and geese – which had long been carried out – was illegal. The molesting of the nest of game birds was prohibited, as was the running at large of bird dogs.

The trapping regulations were meant to insure not only a continuous supply of animals, but also the taking of pelts only when fur was prime and able to fetch top prices.

The regulations applied directly to the white hunter, with certain modifications allowed for northern settlers and for trappers and prospectors when far from civilization.

The Indians were an entirely different matter.

Under the terms of Treaties Five and Six, the Indians were assured of hunting and fishing rights "as long as water flowed and the sun rose." There was a clause which added "on unoccupied Crown land and subject to such regulations as may, from time to time, be made." This raised knotty problems. First and foremost, it is extremely doubtful whether the Indians at that time had any real understanding of the significance of that clause, even had it been explained fully in terms of planned settlement, which it may not have been; for, to do them justice, even the Treaty Commissioners probably did not foresee the rush of settlement which was within forty years to inundate the Indians' hunting ground in the south. Nor could anyone foresee that huge blocks of the northern hunting ground would be set aside as forest reserves and parks which could be gazetted as "occupied."

Secondly, it would take a Philadelphia lawyer to decide whether regulations made by a provincial government (not even visualized when the treaties were drawn up) are of any real effect *vis à vis* the treaties. We must remember that, as most Indians interpreted them, the treaties were made with the Queen. The provincial government might well hold that the parks and so forth were occupied, since they were patrolled by officers of the Crown, but others (including myself) have not held that view.

Always there has been this struggle of good law against a bureaucracy which has become swollen with its own power – a bureaucracy which tends to handle the natives on its own terms of reference, terms which are nearly always at variance with true justice as seen by the natives of this country.

This has brought great hardship to many an Indian. In the teens and twenties, he was at low ebb and spoken of as the "vanishing red man"; had he indeed vanished, it would have saved him much misery, for today he stands with outstretched hands, robbed of the game and fur animals which were his living and, more than that, of his way of life.

And what do we put into those hands? We give him welfare and family allowances and tawdry goods, and comb his hair for lice. We tell him to wash his windows, to put up fly screens. We teach him city values and make him want city life. We give him stones; he wants bread.

We could give him back his fish and game – we would not miss them, for we live in luxury. But we don't. We prefer to sell his game to the tourists, for the demands of opulence from the trade in tourism seem more important to us than the welfare of a nation – the Indian nation; a people who are *not* shiftless, ambitionless and degraded white men, but a nation of hunters and trappers who have had their living taken away.

If all our best-brained economists sat at their desks for the next twenty years they could never evolve an economy of the north which would be half so good as the traditional economy of the Indians. They, and they alone, knew how to use resources and still have them. How close to their hunting culture they lived is apparent to anyone who knows the Cree, Chipweyan or Inuit languages.

I personally had good relations with the Indians in the course of my work, and I always gave them the benefit of the doubt. I realized long ago that the basic reason for the existence of game animals is to provide food and clothing in nonagricultural areas. As the Indians say, the Manito did not create these creatures for "sport."

I have especially discussed the problems of the Indians because we cannot estimate properly the complexities of wildlife protection without recognizing the Indians' legal and moral rights. I think we all understood this in earlier days, but it has been largely forgotten.

It was a year or more before people began to show confidence in the stricter approach, after the years of loose administration, but gradually sportsmen and farmer came around more and more.

At first, I used to hear: "What in the hell do we want with a game guardian? Game will soon be a thing of the past anyway – who cares who gets the last deer?"

I felt surrounded by hostility. I could not foresee that, within a few years, a deer would be pointed out with delight for a youngster to look at; then, such an animal seen from a farmer's binder meant that the man tied up his team while he went for his rifle, even the exigencies of the harvest forgotten.

Even the better informed people showed in their very attempts at friendliness a tongue-in-cheek attitude which seemed to say: "Of course, old boy, we've always done pretty much what we like – after all, it's our country, we built it! (Some of them had; others had been built *by* the country.) We know you have to make a showing and earn your salary and we go along with that – but only so far, you understand.… If you must made a 'pinch,' there are plenty of layabouts and deadbeats who spoil *our* sport by poaching. Pick them up, but not us!"

Worst were the veiled threats of influence in "high place," of "pull" with powers-that-be, and hinted stories of civil servants who had done their duty not wisely, but too well.

The *appearance* of dedication, I could see, would be enough to satisfy the public – but not me.

I felt very lonely.

II

SCHOOLBOYS AND SCAMPS

THE FIRST SUMMER MERGED into fall, and now I felt I had to some extent found my feet.

When my other duties permitted, I had visited many schools to talk about wildlife and point out the beauty of the birds, and the uses of many species of game and furbearers and their value to man. In these talks, I finally became more at ease because of the receptive moods I encountered and the eager interest these children displayed in what I had to say.

I thoroughly enjoyed this informal sort of teaching, which I felt had real value and could be done as and when I had time available, and some of my happiest memories are of those chats in the little country school, with the teacher sitting primly behind her desk. At first she would be diffident, taken aback by my saddle horse and stetson hat, but after a while she would completely thaw out.

I always used the blackboard to depict such things as the posture of woodpeckers, a cross-section of a badger's burrow, or the shape of a pelican bill.

At this time, a campaign against crows had been launched by the government – a campaign I did not feel in sympathy with, since it induced young people to rob crows' nests and bring the eggs to school. Prizes were given to the school collecting the greatest number of eggs. I never believed in the persecution of any bird or animal, and I realized that, with a reward in view, the country boys would tramp through all the prairies and bluffs doing incalculable harm at nesting time, or, worse, would take eggs of other species to palm off as crows' eggs, for few teachers knew one egg from another.

(This is certainly not meant as a criticism of these valiant young women. For about thirty-five dollars per month, they left their homes at seventeen or eighteen to teach the three Rs to the province's children. They often had to live under very uncomfortable conditions; to care for the younger children at all times; to plow through snowdrifts to reach the school and, if necessary, remain blizzard-bound, reading to and caring for their pupils until the parents could get through to pick them up; sometimes they were even called upon to help in fighting prairie fires! No wonder they had no time to study ornithology.)

One day at a school, I counted some two hundred and fifty eggs, of which probably one hundred and fifty were those of crows. The rest included ducks, grouse, killdeer, plover and even bantam eggs.

What particularly caught my eye were four beautiful ovals coloured in ochre and dark purple. They were curlew eggs, eggs of a bird becoming so rare that even the Natural History Museum had none.

I asked which boy had brought them. After some hesitation, a fine, ruddy youngster raised his hand.

"Are these crows' eggs, Tommy?" I asked.

"I *think* they are," said the culprit.

"Did you climb a tree to get them?" I asked relentlessly.

"I don't remember," he stammered.

"Well," I said, "would you remember if I said where you got them?"

"S'pose so," he admitted, rather sullenly.

"Well, Tommy," I said, "you got them from a hollow in the ground on some pasture land, and the bird was big and brown...."

"And it had a great big long beak!" interrupted the boy, his eyes bright with excitement.

"Yes," I said, "that's quite right. Did you think it was a crow?"

"Well, it was awful big...."

"Just so," I replied, "but crows are black, remember that, and they nest in willow bushes or trees. The bird whose eggs you took was a long-billed curlew, and I'll tell you about those birds."

Which I did. (As for the eggs, I confiscated them and they are still among the acquisitions of the Natural History Museum.)

Sometimes, we think we are wasting our time, but thirty-six years later, while I was having a coffee at a roadside counter, a man drove up and sat near me. Suddenly he put down his cup, called me by name, and added, "I've never forgotten the time you lectured me about those curlew eggs, and I've taught all my kids never to disturb any wild thing unless they really have to!"

One day, I got a frantic phone call from a woman far out on the bald prairie. Duck season had started the previous day and her husband and brother-in-law had left that morning for a week's hunting. Early that morning, when she was doing the farm chores, she noticed that a big team of grey percherons which should have been at the pasture bar for their oats were not there. She investigated and found them lying dead in the pasture almost side by side. They seemed to have been shot and she was sure hunters had done it – would I come at once? To my questions, she added that besides herself there were two boys at the farm – her own son aged thirteen and his cousin from town aged twelve, her brother-in-law's boy. As the season opened on a Saturday her brother-in-law, who ran a store in town, had brought his son for the weekend.

Late that afternoon, I arrived at the farm. The woman made a cup of tea and called the boys in. They appeared and said little, and left as quickly and unobtrusively as possible – they were making a play hut in the shelter belt. As I left to look over the horses, I noticed a .22 rifle in the shed corner.

The horses had been shot, all right, with a .22 rifle at short range. I dug into one and extracted a bullet lodged near the heart.

I saw some scruffy tracks on the ground – the pasture was eaten bare, with clumps of grey sage here and there. As I increased my circle I came across a little colony of gopher mounds.

A crow flew away. It had been eating on a gopher drilled with a .22 bullet, and the little animal's tail had been cut off. Schools were giving one cent each for gopher tails in those days. I looked around and found what I wanted – a smoothed-down mound with .22 shells close by and the prints of "sneakers" with corrugated rubber soles. The horses lay about fifty yards away.

I went back to the shelter belt. The boys looked very noncommittal.

I said to one, "Bill, slip back and bring that twenty-two from the shed, will you?"

He left on the run. I took the other boy – by now looking pretty nervous – behind the barn.

"Okay," I said. "Best tell me all about it. I can't waste all day, but I know you kids shot the horses and I have the bullet and the empty shell. Why didn't you just shoot gophers?"

His lips trembled and his eyes wavered and fell.

"Come on, be a man," I said.

"Well, it's like this," he stammered finally, "Dad and Uncle Tony, they was going to open the duck season at Tramping Lake and so we wanted to go. Dad said no. He said we could shoot gophers and pretend they was ducks. We got tired of that, and ... well, we shot the horses, I guess. Are they really *dead*, mister?"

I said, "Yes, they are really dead. But why? Why did you shoot them?"

The boy said, "Well, we got tireda shootin' gophers, so I said to Bill, 'What'd happen if I shot one of the horses?' and Bill says, '*I* don't know Rusty – guess it'd make him flinch a bit. Try it!'

"So I ups and shoots. That horse laid down quite easy. I didn't see no blood nor nothin', so then Bill he let 'tother one have it and he lies down too. We didn't think we hurt them, but Ma says they're dead, and we didn't want to say nothin', but, gee, Mister...."

Just then Bill returned with the twenty-two.

"Only one rifle, Bill?" I asked.

"There's another in the bunkhouse," he said after a bit. He looked at Rusty and didn't need to be told any more. He spoke tearfully. "See, we was only foolin' on account of we couldn't go hunting, see?"

I had a long talk with the mother. I pointed out that a .22 rifle was not a toy and suggested that the guns be confiscated until the boys were sixteen. I told her I had lectured the boys and expected full cooperation from the parents.

The mother finally cheered up. "Those poor horses were purebred and worth a lot of money!" she said. "I reckon those boys'll have to do a lot of stooking to pay for them!"

R.D.S

III

LESSONS AND LEARNING

THE LAST LEAF HAD fallen, and now, on the heels of a grey north wind, the snow had come, and all at once the parklands seemed more open and the view wider. Blue Hill, that famous landmark near Paynton, could be seen even from the north of the river, limned in dusty indigo beneath the snow clouds, or floating in pale cobalt at yellow dawn.

The snow was not deep yet. Not deep enough to cover the low bush nor to conceal the umber-orange of rose hips or the wine-red of bush cranberries, but there was enough to show the tracks of cattle and horses, of grouse and rabbits, and enough, too, for tracking the mule deer which strove to maintain their old range in the face of many changes.

In the south country – south of Township 34 – the season for deer was closed, but here there was still a hunting season, and it was going to take the utmost vigilance to give the protection they needed to does and fawns; otherwise, we should soon write *finis* to the procuring of venison.

I had crossed the "Indian Paint Pot," where every hoofprint of my horse showed red as blood. I had crossed the little bog at the mouth of Big Valley, and seen Pine Island shrouded in the mist of the steamy river, just starting to freeze over.

I had passed several sets of deer tracks, all following the river breaks, and I had seen a big buck lying in his bed among some low bush, for Billy had flicked one ear and shown the white of his eye and I looked where he looked, but the buck never moved and we passed by.

I found a small slough, thick with grass, which lay between two sandhills, and here I turned Billy loose to paw for his dinner and, taking my own sandwiches, brushed the snow off a fallen tree and sat down. It was not cold enough for a fire and I wanted no telltale smoke. My meal finished, I untied Billy's grain bag from the saddle and gave him his ration. As he munched, I smoked my cigarette and watched the play of his strong jaws as he milled the oats, pausing between swallows to look long at some bird or some late fluttering leaf, his jaws silent for better hearing. All being well, he would flick an ear and return to his meal. All the centuries of domestication, I thought, had not dulled the horse's sense of constant vigilance.

"All right, old boy." I bridled him, tightened the cinch, put my foot in the stirrup, and just then I heard a rifle shot, and then another.

Mounted, I turned Billy in the direction from which I judged the sound of the shots came, about a mile and a half west, allowing for the stillness of the winter's day. The rumbling of the discharge continued for some time, rolling and reverberating among the hills and leaping the river to send back an echo from the far banks.

I covered an estimated mile and rode to the top of a sandhill. I could see or hear nothing of note, but Billy looked steadily to the southwest. "Come on," I said, and gave him his head. He slid stiffly down the sloping sidehill, his feet ploughing snow and dry sand together. The short winter day was beginning to close in, and a pale duck-egg green in the northwest heralded colder weather and perhaps more snow.

Soon, we came to a horse track heading south. The rider had evidently been dragging something with his lariat, something that left a deep furrow in the snow and dark stains, which meant blood. If this was a buck, all I would have to do was check a licence, but I wanted to look a little further, and I turned Billy's head and went back on the track. The sandhills were beginning to level out, and less than half a mile away we came to a fence which had been cut. Another hundred yards, and by a bluff in the stubble field, we found where the trail had started. It was a trampled and bloody place in the snow, from which a raven departed on ebony wings, while a whiskey jack merely hopped to one side from the still steaming fat-veined paunch of a deer. The slots of two fawns led away, but they were not in sight.

But to one side was another dent in the snow, more blood and something grey-brown. I knew at once what it was and dismounted, and in a minute was tying the severed head of a young doe to my saddle cantle.

The incoming tracks of the hunter came from the west, the outgoing tracks went south; so, I thought, the two should eventually come together at what surveyors call the point of commencement; unless there was a gate on the far side, the fence had been cut twice.

The tracks met, but it was on an old trail, and here they met a single sleigh track and the signs of a team which had stood for many hours tied to the poplars. The remains of their noon oat sheaves gleamed golden in the snow in the last light, and it was evident that the hunter was a farmer who had led a saddle horse behind his sleigh and hunted out from this temporary "camp."

The doe had been loaded, and now I must follow this sleigh track, which was easy till it pulled on to a main market road, scored by the tracks of many grain sleighs, on which farmers were hauling their wheat to the elevators at the little town ten miles away. It was getting dark, but the track I was following was on top of the others and soon turned off into a farmyard among a general jumble of loose cattle and horse tracks, and I could see these animals standing around a trough at which a heavy-set man was pumping water. He looked up quickly as I approached, but then lowered his head as if he had not seen me. When I bid him good evening, he appeared startled, but I sensed this was mere show.

I told him my name and my business and said I would search his buildings for the meat. He said nothing for a while, then silently led the way to a shed and opened the door. I stepped in and saw the four quarters of a deer hanging from pegs, while below on the floor lay a buck's head, the tongue protruding from the clenched teeth.

"There's my buck, mister," said the man. "Got legal, too. If you want to see my licence, it's in the house."

Nonplussed, I asked him to be good enough to fetch it, and then examined the evidence. The joints were smaller than a buck's should be, but were partly frozen already, for it was now below zero.

I examined the buck's head closely and decided it was from an animal that had been shot some days before, for it was frozen stiff. I put the two neck pieces together and realized they would not fit to the head.

The farmer had returned with the licence, which was in order. I said, "I am seizing this meat and head as evidence of unlawful killing of a doe. You saw the doe head on my saddle, and you must know that I followed the tracks of the meat sleigh here to your farm. I have no other recourse but to lay a charge against you. If you wish to say anything, you are free to do so, but it is fair to give you the usual warning."

This I did, but all he said was, "Do as you please, mister."

I paid him a dollar and a half apiece for gunny sacks to put the meat in and slung the quarters over my saddle. I then wrote out a seizure and receipt and told him to appear next day before the local justice of the peace.

I still had ten miles to ride, but the moon was up, and Billy stepped out willingly enough. I am light, weighing not much more than a boy, and the extra sixty or so pounds of meat meant little to the big bay.

All the way, I conned over the matter, convinced that the meat belonged to the doe, and reminding myself of what the Act said: "Where a game guardian is satisfied that an offence has been committed, it shall be his duty to lay whatever charges, etc., etc."

Billy was glad to see the livery barn, and soon I was eating ham and eggs at the B.C. Café. I had already dropped the meat off at the justice of the peace's house, and now I went around to see him. He was a most genial type, but well aware of his responsibilities. He had been a pioneer of the district, but now in his later years he rented out his farm land and was engaged in clerical work in the village. He produced an Information and Complaint form and I drew up the charge.

Of course, I had not *seen* my man shoot the doe. Perhaps he would claim that some other person had actually done that, and that he had chased this unknown party off and just possessed himself of the deer. But the Act said: "No one shall hunt, shoot, shoot at, trap, kill or *take* any animal which is protected, etc."

So my charge read: "That A.B. of the District of C. at or near such a quarter section, on or about such a date, did unlawfully *take* a female big game animal, to wit: a mule deer doe, contrary to the provisions of the Game Act of Saskatchewan."

"Hmm," said the JP, "this case seems okay," and signed the form. He added, "I know that fellow pretty well, and he's always been a poacher. I hear he takes deer all the year around. In fact, my grandchildren were telling me only the other day that his kids bring venison sandwiches to school. Seems they get tired of them and trade the other kids for doughnuts and apples. You understand this is common gossip, but no one wants to report these things – 'specially where kids are concerned – and I'm mighty glad the department has sent a man to look around. Do a power of good."

He puffed his pipe for a while. "Incidentally," he said, "that's my land he was hunting on, and my fence he cut, and that makes me mad, for I ordered him off a couple of times already. However, I musn't bring that in, 'cos they'd say I was biased, and I want to take the case because then he'll *know* what I *think*, anyway."

As I left for the hotel, I wished I had investigated more thoroughly – it was snowing hard, and I knew all tracks would be covered by morning.

I lost that case. It was the first and the last I lost in fifteen years. But I learned a lot.

The man called a lawyer up from North Battleford. He really hammered my evidence to shreds. He asked if I could prove that the sleigh track I followed had not pulled *right through* the man's barnyard and across a field beyond which lay several other farms? Could I produce the rifle? Could I show the court the horses? Had I the rope which must have dragged the carcass? Here were four quarters of a deer. Who knew what sex? The accused had a buck's head to show – what piffle to carp about an exact fit where head and neck met after freezing, dragging and heaven knows what else. Exhibit A (my doe head) could have come from anywhere – Perhaps the game warden carried it as stock-in-trade!

Over and above all, his client was charged with "unlawfully taking," and *that* – he produced a Statute of Definitions – *that* was theft, and very well taken care of in the Criminal Code of Canada; and he, a lawyer, was only too glad to say on behalf of his client that any provincial law dealing with theft was *ultra vires*. "And now, Your Worship, here is my client's valid licence, which I produce as evidence of his good faith." And he laid it on the JP's table.

"I ask for this case to be dismissed."

It was, but at least I had sufficient presence of mind, before returning the licence to the accused, to write on it: "One mule deer," with the date.

Since the licence called for two (buck) deer, this would only allow one more, and I was determined to keep a watch that he did not exceed that.

The meat was returned, and the accused left a court now fallen strangely silent, for this case had been well attended and before the opening there had been a good deal of chat.

Thus did I receive a salutary lesson in the careful gathering of every scrap of evidence and in the presentation of a case which could stand fast before the assaults of the honourable members of the legal profession.

I heard a good deal of postmortem chat. A lost case can be bad, but I heard at least one remark that took some of the sting away. I was eating my supper at the BC, and some farmers were talking in another booth. Said one, "Can't see how A.B. got off like that. Why, everyone knew he got that doe same as he's been doing for years."

"Oh hell, you can't tell with lawyers," said another. "That young chap did alright, considering. A guy like A.B.'s been jumping ahead of the law so long he's experienced, and the guardian did his best. Everyone knew he was the only man telling the truth in that court. He traced it step by step, and I can see it all, because that's just the way A.B. always does. But you bet he'll watch out from now on. An' while we're on the subject, I reckon we all better be more careful. Suits me, anyway – I hate to see the game going the way it has been."

On my return to Battleford, I found a letter from the Baljennie country about thirty miles southeast complaining that a certain party was trapping muskrat out of season on a large slough near Swan Lake which the complainant trapped legally every spring. He wrote that if I made a patrol, I would probably catch this man in the act.

At that time we were doing our utmost to stop the trapping of muskrat in the fall and early winter when the pelts had not reached their prime and were therefore worth much less. In addition, opening of the muskrats' houses and runs in the late fall allowed much damage by freezing.

Next morning, therefore, I saddled the buckskin, which had been enjoying a good rest, and set out. The sun was not yet up, but the sky glowed in the southeast and the broad shoulders of the Eagle Hills loomed dark and sharply outlined. The old Saskatoon Trail had been little used, but the snow was still not deep enough to make hard travelling, and Buck pulled on the bit and blew his nose sharply in the frosty air.

I was clad in winter riding dress: moccasins over three pairs of wool socks, Angora chaps, buffalo coat, fur hat and mitts.

This was what I loved: the crisp early dawn; the muffled thud of hooves in the snow; the heart-warming willing trot, with the strong shoulders moving beneath the winter hair and the mane streaming backwards; the frost-laden trees, blue and fuzzy against the now golden sky, and the swift flight of a ruffled grouse from the trail-side with the wind from its scurrying wings sending the frost-rime floating down to form little dimples in the uncharted snow.

By noon, we had made it up through the timber to the big lonely slough which lay so white and still between the grey-green banks of poplar and the patches of low red willow which rimmed the shore. Clumps of sere and frozen rushes margined the snow-covered ice of the centre, and among those clumps I could see the darker mounds of muskrat houses – many of them.

There was no one in sight and it was very quiet, until a moving band of chickadees arrived to look at us briefly and then scour through the willows in cheerful company.

From where I was, I could see the telltale tracks of a trapper linking up the muskrat houses of moss and waterweed, and could see too the darker gashes showing where they had been chopped into for the setting of traps.

I reckoned that the trapper would start his evening round in another hour, so, having led Buck into a heavy grove, I waited, keeping warm as best I might. I had not long to wait, and caught the fellow red-handed with two rats in his pouch. We then lifted the rest of his traps – thirty – and bagged them, and with some protest from Buck I fastened them over the saddle.

It seemed that the man's place was only half a mile away, so I took him back there and seized another eight or ten rats which were drying on their stretchers – yesterday's catch, I took them to be.

He said he'd sold all the pelts he had taken previously, but refused to say to whom, as he would not be a party to getting anyone "in wrong." It was now only about 4 p.m., and Maymont and a JP were just over the nob – perhaps seven miles away – so I told him to mount his pony and come along.

We rode silently for a bit, but finally he spoke. "Say, mister," he said, "this will go pretty hard with me, I guess."

"Oh, I don't know," I replied. "That's up to the court – not me."

"Yes, but you see...." He stumbled a bit. "You see, it's the second offence for me."

"How come?" I asked.

"Well, you see, two years ago I got pinched for trapping on Sunday."

"I see," I said. "Who pinched you?"

"Mountie. Someone squealed and he caught me...."

"Where was this?" I asked.

"Right along the river. Mountie drove by in his car and there I was with a couple of weasels and a coyote."

We relapsed into silence.

Ourselves fed and the horses put into the livery barn, I took my man up to the JP's house. He'd just finished supper.

I said to my man, "Want to go down to the pool hall for fifteen minutes? We'll be ready for you then – and mind, no tricks. Be back on time or I'll be looking for you."

"Okay," he said, and lumbered off.

I turned to the JP. "I am going to charge this man," I explained, "but, first of all, he said you'd convicted him a year ago. Could I have some particulars?"

"You sure can," the JP replied, and shuffled through a file. "Here you are. Record of conviction against J.W. – hmm – a year ago – no, two years. Trapping on Sunday. Section Twenty-four, Game Act."

"If you don't mind, I'd like to have a copy of that," I said, and took out a pad and pencil. I also took the Game Act from my saddle bag.

"The section dealing with hunting on Sunday," I said, "says nothing about *fur bearers*.... The seizures, you say, were in this case two weasels and a coyote. Who signed the charge, by the way?"

"Oh, the neighbour who complained," answered the JP.

I went on. "Well, as I was saying, the word 'trap' is here but it doesn't apply. The act says: 'No person shall hunt, trap, take, shoot at or wound or kill any *game* bird or animal mentioned in this Act on the first day of the week, commonly known as Sunday.' I'm afraid a mistake has been made that will have to be put right. We hope soon to have a special Fur Act and that will help to avoid confusion. I have no doubt this man specially thought he was doing wrong, but that makes no difference."

"Gosh," said the JP, "What a bloomer. It's not to my credit, but I agree with you. He was fined twenty-five dollars, too, and that family isn't rich."

"Thank you," I said, and just then the accused came back.

We opened the court and the accused pleaded guilty. His traps were confiscated and he was fined twenty dollars and costs, which he paid at once, seemingly glad that it wasn't more. Anyway, he was one meal ahead, as I had paid for his supper.

He said goodnight and went to the barn for his horses, saying, "I'll be a bit late milking the cows – but perhaps with any luck my wife will have done that."

Next morning, I called on a local storekeeper who dealt in furs, and found my fellow's name opposite an entry for some weasels and a mink, so I questioned him pretty thoroughly about... fall rats?

Not being satisfied, I made a pretty thorough search of store and sheds. Nothing turned up till I went into a dark old buggy shed and there, under the seat of a two-horse cutter, I found a bulky package containing what I was looking for – muskrats.

When my report went in, it was accompanied by all seizures and also by all particulars of the unfortunate case two years ago, and in due course my "client" received a handsome letter from the attorney general enclosing a cheque for twenty-five dollars!

Within a week I was investigating another case of illegal killing of deer after the close of the season. It was shortly before Christmas, and I received information from a farmer near Whitkow that a certain party had killed three deer – two of them does – on an island in the lake. The meat was supposed to be cached in an old ice house on this island. My informant added that Nick, the farmer's hired man, had been involved in a wages dispute with his employer, which had led to an angry break, and in revenge or in spite this man had told my informant all about the deer just before he left the district. As this man himself had a bad record, the letter added, perhaps I had better check with the police.

I did so, and found that Nick had been sentenced only a few days before for theft of wheat, and was at present serving a term in the Prince Albert jail.

The sergeant said that he would prove a poor witness, and it would not be worth while to bring him down for the purpose.

"However," he said, "I think a patrol up there might do a lot of good. You remember that case last year which you assisted us with? That wasn't the first murder up there, and there are a few people who'd like to see you again – Tom Guest, for example. Now there's a real good citizen, and he was complaining not long ago that certain people hunt whenever it suits them and have made a few cracks about you. I'd call on Tom if I were you, but don't advertise it – someone might take revenge on him, and he has to live there."

The upshot of this was that I found the meat in the hut as reported – not a head nor a hide, but enough odd quarters of meat to account for at least three deer and probably more.

Coming back, I found a doe head frozen in the ice by the shore. It was partly eaten, and had probably been dragged there by a coyote and had subsequently frozen in. I had no ax, but I dismounted and was able to cut away a good part of it with my hunting knife. It wasn't much good as evidence, but it did give colour to the story that someone had killed a doe.

Dry wood had recently been cut along the sleigh trail which crossed the ice from the mainland into the wooded part of the island. I followed this track by a devious route along the mainland shore, and it ended at the buildings of the man under suspicion.

Having ridden to the district by night, I was reasonably sure that no one but Tom Guest knew I was about. I had carefully avoided making contact with my informant, in order not to involve him, so I should have been in a position to surprise my man.

I found him doing chores at the barn, and he showed his guilt and concern. I made him stay with me while I searched the premises. On the kitchen table was a cold venison stew, and in the granary a small piece of frozen meat and a shrunken buck's head with a good spread of antlers.

These looked to me like props – something to show to any snooper. I knew he'd had a licence during the season, and these items he could swear quite conscientiously were parts of a legally taken animal.

However, by now I was getting to know the tricks of the trade. If this man had brought back meat from the hut just a few days before it certainly would not be in the granary. So I marched my man over to a threshing separator at the far end of the yard on ground where the snow was well beaten down by cattle. Opening the side door to the straw-blower I reached in and brought out a quarter of venison, and then another. They were frozen, but not yet blackened. I realized this was a recent kill. The suspected man uttered not a word.

I next examined the wood pile. The empty sleigh which had brought the last load still sat beside the mound of crooked poplar poles. The bunk stakes leaned crookedly and the log-chain lay across the reach. On several of the poles, I found blood stains and, stuffed into the woodpile, some gunny sacks with fat, blood and a few hairs clinging to the inside. I took these for evidence and, with the bucksaw which lay there, I cut the billets from the poles where they showed the stains.

The quarters of meat at the separator plainly showed the impression of gunny sacks.

Making up the story in my own mind, it appeared that, about a week before, this man had gone to the island, cut a load of wood and shot a doe. My timing took account of the fact that the track was not more than a week old.

He made one mistake in a perfect setup. He said he had only killed one deer on his licence. He was entitled to two, and with his reputation he would have done better to acknowledge a full bag. He couldn't alter his statement, as he had sent his licence back to the department at the close of the season (as the law required) and had marked down "one mule deer" – but I didn't know all this at the time, and my concern was that in court he would change his story.

I might not be able to prosecute him successfully regarding the meat cached on the island, but I did have a very good chance of conviction in this later development. It was too late now for him to produce another buck head, and law required that evidence of sex must be preserved.

I had one more little investigation to make, so I went to the house again. His .30-.30 Winchester was in the bedroom, along with a half-empty box of shells, both of which I confiscated.

Finally, I went down into the cellar. On the shelves I found about sixty quart bottles of canned deer meat. The woman of the house was a tidy soul, and had scribbled that year's date on all of them. Here was altogether too much meat for one buck head, and I took a bottle as evidence. These people, incidentally, had over a hundred head of cattle and hogs, besides several granaries full of wheat; they were not starving pioneer settlers at all.

I told the man to appear in town on such a day. Would he come without a summons?

"Yes," he said.

I then had to hire a team and sleigh and collect my exhibits. They hadn't the nerve to move the meat in the cellar, but when I went to the island I found another team and sleigh just ahead of me. They were neighbours, and had evidently been communicated with by the accused in an effort to get rid of the evidence in the hut.

As we drew alongside, I said, "Hello! Going for wood?"

"Yep," replied the teamster. "We're 'most out, and it's going to get colder, I think."

Well, I'd given him a way out, but that's the first time I ever saw a man go for wood with no axe and a grain box on his sleigh!

The day of the trial came. I had telephoned the Regina office and been sent the incriminating licence.

Court was being held at the RCMP divisional office. The accused arrived with a lawyer who was noted for getting his clients off. I prayed fervently that my evidence would hold.

While the magistrate was getting ready and fussing with his papers, I noticed a man in the top bunk of the night-cell. I presumed he was sleeping off a drunk. He was lying on his back with one arm over his face.

The court was opened and the charge read. The accused, through his lawyer, pleaded not guilty.

"Here goes," I said to myself, "we probably won't get this chap on the stand, and that may be awkward.

However, I started my evidence – my authority, the section, the time, the place, and so on. The lawyer looked like the cat ready to finish off the rat.

I was presenting my exhibits when, during a pause, I heard the drunk let out a groan and change his position. He now turned his back, and I could see he was thickset, youngish, and had a head of black curly hair, and I recognized him as a well-known local character by the name of Mike.

The accused and his lawyer turned, too, at the groan. I don't think they'd seen the man before, for the basement of the building was large and the cells gloomy.

I noticed that the accused plucked at his lawyer's sleeve and whispered something.

The legal gentleman shook his head slightly, and heard me out to the end of my case for the Crown. Then he stepped forward, and requested a five-minute adjournment.

"What for?" asked the magistrate.

"My client wishes to consult me."

"Well," said His Worship, "you've had lots of time for that. However, yes. Gentlemen, this court stands adjourned for five minutes."

The accused and his advisor consulted by the door. Then I was beckoned over. The lawyer said, "Officer, if my client pleads guilty will you recommend a minimum fine?"

"Sorry, I can't do that," I said. "This is too serious a case, and His Worship must decide for himself."

"Pity," commented the lawyer dryly. I wondered what this meant. It had a threatening sound.

Another deep sigh from the cells.

The court was called to order.

The lawyer was speaking: "… client begs leave to alter his plea to guilty."

It was soon over. The fine *was* the minimum – fifty dollars – but considering costs and legal fees it was a good deterrent.

Outside the accused grinned and said, "No hard feelings, officer?"

"Why should there be?" I replied. "But why did you suddenly plead guilty?"

"Why? Why?" He seemed puzzled. "'Cos I knew that if you'd gone to all the trouble of bringing Mike down as a witness, I was sunk!"

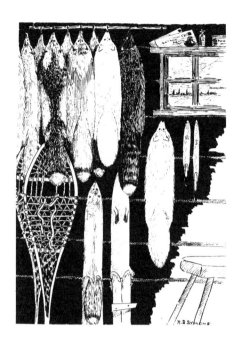

IV

RISKS AND RAMBLES

THE MUSKRAT SEASON OPENED in March, and there was much to do by way of checking up. The prairie sloughs all held their quota of small fur bearers, and Indians and Metis would wander for miles by wagon, camping now here, now there. The Indians, under the provisions of the treaties, did not require licences, but Metis were supposed to have that two-dollar square of cardboard.

Mostly, these people gave little trouble, but there were sometimes questions of trespass to consider. A great many – in fact most – of the old-time ranchers and farmers who operated on a larger scale were glad to let their old acquaintances of mixed blood, or their neighbours from the reserves, camp and trap on their land, and there was seldom trouble in this connection.

But a majority of the settlers were relatively newcomers, and more were coming in every year to purchase CPR land, much of which had lain open for years and had always been considered free trapping areas by the semi-nomadic natives.

These newcomers had little appreciation of the old ways, and none at all of the traditional way of life of the trapping fraternity whose country they had invaded. Therefore, these settlers complained bitterly of people camping on their land or taking a few animals which they looked upon as a perquisite.

I did all I could for both sides and, on the whole, the situation resolved itself without undue friction.

Much more troublesome was the rivalry between the white trappers in the larger marshes on the fringe of the northern woods. Claims and counterclaims to trapping grounds were filed with monotonous regularity.

A common thing was for a man to run his rivals off a marsh on the pretext that he held a trapping lease from the department or a fur farm permit which permitted riparian control of the area. One such case which required investigation was in the northeastern part of my district.

A farmer from there wrote to me that a certain man, whom I shall call Luke, had driven him at gunpoint from his own land, which bordered on a large swamp are. Not only that, but Luke had taken up this farmer's traps and "confiscated" them. My informant went on to say that Luke told him he had a fur farm licence on this swamp, and that no one but he was allowed to trap there. He had added that he intended to keep a strict patrol.

When the farmer tried to suggest getting in touch with the department, Luke had said hotly that *he* was the game guardian there, and what he said went.

This promised to be interesting, and I rode the seventy odd miles in a day, arriving at my informant's under the cover of dusk. After a hearty supper, he took me about a mile to the home of a neighbour, who gave me a statement to the effect that his land also bordered on the swamp; that he had trapped there for some fifteen years; that, two years ago, he too had been ordered off by Luke and told the same story; then, when he went next morning to lift his traps, he found them gone, and two rifle bullets whistled over his head, apparently shot from the other side of the marsh – the side on which Luke lived.

I tucked the two statements carefully in my tunic. Luke's name was not on my list of fur leases, and I felt quite sure the man was bluffing.

Next morning early, I detoured around the swamp, keeping well back in the brush, and finally rode into the littered yard in which stood Luke's small cabin. No one was about, not even a dog, but the door, in keeping with tradition, had no lock. After knocking and getting no response, I entered. The cabin was neat, as bachelor's quarters usually are, and equipped with a table, a cupboard, a cook stove and a double bed neatly covered with a couple of three-and-a-half point Hudson Bay blankets in brilliant red.

I made a cigarette and sat on the bed to consider whether I should wait for the occupant to return, which might not be for hours as the stove was still warm from his breakfast, or take a ride around.

I decided that waiting was the best policy, and leaned back on the bed. It was then I felt something knobby under the blankets and threw them back. Here was a small arsenal, and I drew the weapons forth, one by one. First, a double-barrelled twelve-gauge shotgun. I broke it, and there were two shells in the breech. I laid them aside and replaced the gun. Next was a Model 1895 .30-.30 Winchester, its magazine full and a shell in the breech. This, too, I unloaded, the shells popping out to land with a thud on the red cloth, where they shone and twinkled in brassy bravado. Finally, a .32 Smith and Wesson revolver, every chamber full. These shells joined the others.

All weapons unloaded, I looked for a place to put the shells. Just what I wanted was an array of Comfort tobacco tins on a high shelf. Investigating, I found nuts and bolts in one of them, another held the spare parts of a gasoline lamp and several were empty. Into one of the latter I packed the shells and then put the can at the bottom of the pile. A box of .22 long shells I also concealed.

The bed remade, there was no sign of interference, and, satisfied so far, I went outside and found what I wanted – a cache in which lay about eighty muskrat skins tied in the usual bundles of ten, plus another dozen odd skins drying on stretchers. Behind the cache was a pile of dried and skinned muskrat bodies.

There were only two traps to be found, both defective, so I reckoned that Mr. Luke was putting to good use all his own, as well as those he had taken from his neighbours.

I went back into the cabin. I was pretty hungry, so looked around and found some tea and some kindling and was soon enjoying a cup. This may sound funny, but at that time and in these circumstances every man's cabin was open, and foe was as welcome to food as friend. No matter how angry a man might be at being apprehended, it would never have occurred to him that there should be any ill will over a cup of tea!

I had tied my horse well back from the cabin in a bunch of spruce and poplar, and when Luke finally came in sight I was in the cabin. I saw him through the small grimy window and, as he strode up to the door (the fire being long out) there was nothing to warn him I was within. He pushed the door open and, bent as he was under the burden of a gunny sack containing freshly caught rats and a few steel traps, he didn't notice me as he stood his .22 rifle by the door jamb.

Then he twisted sideways to let the sack fall heavily to the floor, and in that second, unseen by him, I set the rifle outside, opening the bolt as I did so, to see the head of a detonated shell. It was a single-shot rifle, harmless until he could reload.

This little stir caused him to look up, but, before he could speak, I announced myself and the purpose of my visit. I then asked him to produce his fur farm lease if he had one.

Not a muscle of his face moved and, for a moment, he just stared at me. I sized him up. About forty or forty-five, heavily set; powerful, I judged; grizzled hair and sky-blue eyes. A skookum man – and I kept well back and was glad of my side arms.

Finally he said, "Okay," and made a quick stride for the bed. The blankets were turned back in a jiffy and he seized the Winchester.

"Steady," I said. "I have unloaded all your firearms."

This changed his thoughts, and he checked the Winchester and threw it to the floor with a curse, then the shotgun, then the revolver. Finally, he spoke.

"What in hell do you mean by stealing my shells? Them shells cost money and I need 'em. Come on, where did you put them? I want them. I got enemies, see?"

I told him they were safe and he would probably get them back, but in the meanwhile I had some questions to ask. There was something rather comical, and yet pathetic and also a little frightening, in the way he searched that place, muttering, for his precious shells. (He seemed to have forgotten the twenty-two.) This, at all events, did have the effect of taking his mind off his first intentions which, I am sure, were hostile to a degree.

The upshot was that I arrested him, seized the arsenal and the bag of traps and soft furry bodies, and escorted him to the nearest town, where I put him in a cell to await the coming of the local JP in half an hour or so.

Meanwhile, I wired Regina, and soon had a reply. This man had applied for a fur farm lease three years before, but was refused on the grounds that too many settlers had trapped there before he had come to the district.

He had also been sent a letter of warning by registered mail two years before as a result of a report that he had claimed to be the possessor of a lease. The wire closed by saying that, should I need copies of any of this correspondence and a man to swear to them, I could wire them again and put off the prosecution.

I did not think this would be necessary. Luke was charged under the Criminal Code for possession of an unregistered revolver, as well as for possession of stolen traps (he did have a trapper's licence).

I went back to Luke's cabin to pick up the furs and traps, which was a long job and required many miles of walking over the ice of the still frozen marsh in the footsteps of the trapper, which went from muskrat house to muskrat house. He was told that under his licence he was permitted to trap only on that portion of marsh adjacent to his own land. This was a fractional quarter that he had purchased from the CPR, and the only improvements were his house and a small barn. He had evidently acquired this area simply as an excuse to claim the marsh.

Luke was promptly convicted and, after his fine was paid, those traps which bore his mark were returned to him, which was only fair as the man had to live. On my recommendation, the JP also allowed him one-third of the pelts, as he had a trapper's licence, and the balance was divided between the other men who lived on the marsh.

This may all sound rather casual, but at that time we still believed in private enterprise and, so long as no injury or murder had been done, we had perhaps a sneaking respect for a man's efforts to preserve his empire, be that empire real or imaginary.

It was, perhaps, fortunate for all concerned that it was only later that I learned that Luke was considered a dangerous man. He had mauled a fellow pretty badly in a lumber camp and had at that time received treatment for mental distress!

I had run into the usual number of fairly mild infractions and handled them, I thought, satisfactorily. In several cases when I encountered infractions (such as Sunday hunting) before any game was taken, I let the offenders off with a warning, but I pointed out that the carrying of a gun in the vicinity of game was *prima facie* evidence that they *were* hunting rather than just walking across a field to return a borrowed weapon. I also let them know that I might suddenly turn up at any time when least expected. In two cases, I had prosecuted and convicted the offenders, but these were cases where guilt was so obvious that pleas of "guilty" were entered. In such cases, the game taken was confiscated, but guns were returned by the court.

But now, the game bird season was coming in, and there would be no time for cosy chats in school, for there would be long days and nights of patrolling from wetland to wetland at daylight and at dusk when the wildfowl flights were on, and through the heat of the day the side roads and trails to watch, for here was where the hunters obtained most of their ruffed grouse and prairie chickens. (Properly called short-tailed grouse, but I shall use the homey vernacular.)

I made it an invariable rule never to interrupt a shoot unless it was necessary, for it would serve no useful purpose to spoil the sport of a law-abiding man. So if a party was "pitted in" for geese I would wait until the shoot was over, and then check licences and guns (some types were not allowed), as well as bag limits and species. Some hunters were very bad with regard to the latter, and if no ducks came over would shoot a muskrat in the water or a gull on the wing in total disregard of ethics and the law.

One one occasion, I had just checked on a democrat-load of ten hunters who had distributed themselves among the reeds on a narrows between two small lakes. I had checked their licences and found them in order. As the ducks would soon be on the move, I got out of the way, warning them that a small flock of pelicans was on one of the lakes and might possibly come over and that these were not to be molested because they were on the protected list.

I had hardly got to my horse when "Bang! Bang!" came from behind the bushes. Turning, I saw a fine white pelican come crashing down. I returned to the scene, and saw the leader of the party picking up the bird and heard him say, "Just what I wanted! I'll have it stuffed for my den."

Now this man occupied a very high position and was one of those who had hinted to me that he and the government were "like that," but who had opined that it was a crime the way the Metis and Indians went after the game.

He turned in real surprise as he heard me approach through the brittle reeds, and dropped the bird so that it looked a mere heap of white among the herbage.

"Hello, Officer!" (I didn't like the honeyed "Officer.") "Hello, Officer! Just got me a nice snow goose. Say, d'you ever take a little of you know what?" Here, he produced a "micky" and uncorking it, "Sure a good thing to keep out the wet… or if it's too hot," he added hastily, for it was one of those sultry September days.

I shook my head.

"Well, I'll just have a little myself – but say, no one's stand-offish here, and you're perfectly safe with us boys, ain't he?" He turned to the others, who agreed.

I picked up the bird.

"Your gun, sir, please," I said.

"My gun? Say, no one's ever taken my gun – what for, anyway?"

"I think you know," I replied. "You have shot a bird – a pelican – that I had warned you about. You will be charged with an infraction of the Migratory Birds Act. And now, your gun."

I hardened my voice, and he let me take his gun from a somewhat limp hand.

"Now," I continued, "I have your name and you are known to me. I can arrest you now and take you to town" – he tried to interrupt, but I well knew there must never be an argument, and I held up my hand and went on – "and bring your case before Mr. Johnson on summary conviction; or, if you behave reasonably, you may appear on a summons, which will be served on you. That's all."

"Well, say," he said, "you sure are a hard man – what's the idea? Can't I pay my fine right now? That'll save you a lot of trouble, won't it?"

I replied, "I am not judge and jury, simply a game guardian. I have no authority to fine you, and you are at perfect liberty to plead not guilty if you wish."

He gave in. Rather ruefully, he asked if he would get his gun back, and I told him that would be at the discretion of the court. He then asked if a summons was necessary, so long as he promised to appear when notified. Summonses, he said, were the darndest things, and you had to pay for them. So I told him that so long as he appeared (and I knew he would), I would not have him served.

I left them all very embarrassed. In a couple of days, this gentleman appeared in court, pleaded guilty, and was fined and his gun returned. By the way, he was a JP himself, and later became one of my best backers. As he said one time, "You see, everyone was doing it, but, when we seen you made no exceptions, I got to thinking what a good thing it really was, and when you got A., and then B., and a few others who thought themselves immune, I felt a lot better."

It was on one of these patrols that I nearly lost Billy. I had come from the north and was heading for the bush country south of the Battle River, angling through the unfenced sandhills towards the ford which would lead me to a trail that wound up over the steep southern slope. It was the afternoon of a golden October day and the country was at its loveliest, the leaves of the poplars glowing like golden guineas, the small lakes smiling to the blue sky and the valley hazy with smoke from burning brush piles.

I checked one small party of hunters who were shooting prairie chicken until the evening duck flight.

Near the ford, a mule deer doe with two well-grown fawns moved away with the springing bounce of their kind. The water was cool and sweet, and Billy stood hock deep in the stream to slake his thirst. A small party of widgeons, disturbed at their siesta, took wing and disappeared around the bend, whistling.

Billy grunted up the far bank and then settled into his swingy walk, following a dim cowpath leading south by west. I reckoned I was about a mile from the trail I wanted. We climbed steadily for a mile and then the path turned abruptly to the right following the edge of an old oxbow pond, with heavy timber on the right and a typical rocky bank on the left. The curving valley became narrower and narrower, and more and more grown over with tangled slough grass. Finally, all that separated me from the open bench was a small patch of suspiciously green vegetation hemmed on either side with big closely grown poplars and hoary tangled willows.

"What about it, Billy?" I said. "Looks like it might be a spring, but go on, anyway...."

Billy stepped forward quite confidently on a loose rein. The ground seemed perfectly hard. Then, all at once, he broke through. I was off in a second and pulled on the bridle. My feet were on firm ground, but Billy, after one or two terrific heaves, could not free his front legs and sank slowly in thick mud until only his neck and head and a strip of back still showed.

I put the lariat, with a bowline, round his neck, and a piece of log under his throat. I gathered all the brush and dead wood I could find and packed it close around him. I had heard a dog bark from above just before the horse went down, and now I heard it again.

I scrambled up the bank and headed for the sound. I came to a trail and, as the woods thinned, I saw the outline of some buildings on the top of the hill about a quarter of a mile away. I slipped through a pasture fence and, following another cow path, trudged up to the buildings from the rear.

A big yellow dog came prancing towards me, growling deep but waving the plume of his tail, and I stood my ground till he sniffed at me. Then, as if satisfied, he trotted through the barnyard and up to the house, scratching at the door and looking from it to me as if he wanted in. I knocked. No reply. I tried again. Still silence. I searched around the farm buildings. No one in sight. I listened intently for the sound of a binder. Dusk was falling and the fields were silent and empty.

Desperately, I searched for a rope, a chain, or some horses and harness. The barn stalls were empty. I looked in the shop, where every farmer repairs his implements and stores his tools. Good and hooray! There was a set of heavy blocks and tackle with plenty of inch rope – haying equipment. My friend the dog had accompanied me on my quest, sniffing at everything and watching my movements with shining eyes, as if he too were in this novel game.

The dusk had deepened as I clumped awkwardly down the pasture slopes into the deep, shrouded valley, with the rope trailing and the heavy blocks bumping. I made it through the fence, cut off by the trail into the woods, and half fell, half slid, down the short steep bank, fearful of what I might encounter. But, O blessed relief! There was my friend's solemn white blaze still reflecting the last of the light, and a soft whinny to greet me.

I couldn't get the rope around Billy's body, but I knew the horn and cinches of the stout stock saddle would hold; so over the horn I slipped a loop, adjusted my ropes and, with one block fastened to a stout old poplar, I very gradually got the horse out. Each time I gained half an inch, I tied fast, and then packed more brush and sticks around the horse. Finally I was able to get first one and then his other front leg out and stretched forward, in the position a horse assumes as he gets up from the ground. Then one final, frantic heave, and Billy took heart and used those legs. With a "plop" that put him on his knees, he had his hind-quarters out, and then, with another heave, he was on his feet and on firm ground.

He was mud to his eyes, stinking from the bog, and his legs trembled from the cold spring water which was rapidly filling the hollow which had so nearly engulfed him. I took the rigging off and began quickly to scrape the mud off with a stick, still weary and panting myself and wet with sweat. I gathered dry grass and rubbed his legs and cleaned the green slime from his mouth and eyes.

And all the time, the wise old dog trotted back and forth between us and the boghole, sniffing at the evil-smelling mud, leaving his possessive sign on the neighbouring trees, or raising his long muzzle to Billy's head as if he understood the whole thing.

I loaded the blocks and ropes on the saddle and led Billy as far as the now dim trail to get the circulation back into his legs. The mud began to dry on his tail and rattled as he walked. At the trail, I mounted and said goodbye to that innocent-looking valley as the last rays of light gilded the tops of the poplars and an owl, out early for his hunting, swooped silently across a glade.

This time, I followed the trail and came around to the buildings from the front. I saw a sudden spurt of light reveal a window. I heard a voice call "Sport?" and my canine companion leapt forward. I heard the jingling of harness and a thud of hooves as a team was driven to the barn, bulking tall and dark in the background. I dropped Billy's lines at the door and knocked.

A young woman answered.

"I'm very sorry," I said, "I got my horse bogged down just over the hill, and I'm afraid I just helped myself to your block and tackle, which I wish to return. I'm the game guardian."

"Oh, goodness! Do come in! Did you get him out? Oh, yes, I see you did – are you both all right?"

"Yes, thanks," I replied. "We made it!"

Early in the season, I started on a patrol which would take me to Midnight Lake, then by way of the English River to Pike's Peak and Waseca, and finally northwest to the Manito Lake area and southward by Wilkie to Battleford.

The snow was nearly gone, the lake ice was melting and spring was in the air. It was the season for the fur dealers to be picking up beaver and muskrat, the season for spring shooting (long since prohibited), and also the time for the return of the birds to the north land.

At Midnight Lake, I ran into a hide buyer who travelled by pickup Ford. I searched him pretty thoroughly, but I found nothing until I opened some beef hides, within which were five beaver pelts.

Having taken care of that case, I went on next day, by way of a wagon road, to Turtle Lake, to find what I expected from the tracks of narrow wagon tires – an Indian camp. It was a camp of three tall tipis and two ordinary tents, and the head man was my friend Meesto, he of the long white braid (something uncommon in an ethnic group not given to white hair even late in life). Others in the camp were Oosecap (who grinned like a skinned beaver), young Red Thunder and Josie (or O'chipwayo), all of whom had brought their wives and families.

One really handsome Indian girl, a niece of Oosecap's and not yet married, had just finished braiding her hair, and now threw these braids, joined at the end with a bit of red thread, over her head to fall behind her (a gesture which usually indicated that some stooping posture was in the offing).

I saw her pick up a skin-scraper, but Oosecap made a motion with his hand and she sat down with some of the other girls.

A dog made for my legs growling, but old Mrs. Meesto grabbed a club and beat him off with a loud "*Awas atim!*" and he slunk away.

Greetings passed, as old Meesto asked if the *moswokimāw* (myself) was going to stop them from hunting? I said no, but they must remember to keep to the forest and away from the white men's land. This was gravely acquiesced to, for, said the spokesman, it was not safe for an Indian to be around the settlements any more – white men might mistake him for a deer!

I asked, was the hunting good? Yes, pretty good. Did I wish to see for myself? I was shown a moose hide, which was being made into buckskins, laced to the stretcher back in the poplar woods, partly scraped and nearly ready to be tanned by smoke to that sweet-smelling, velvety tobacco brown which is the pride of the Cree.

The meat was hanging in strips from the drying racks beside the narrow creek – no waste here. But a doe was being skinned, and her unborn fawn had already been skinned to make a medicine bag, which brought a rebuke from me. I told them their rights were one thing, but they would be empty rights if they did not stop killing females. Somewhat embarrassed, the old chief said he quite agreed, but some of the young men did not look too closely – also, he said, even the young ones must have their medicine bags.

Leaving their camp, I stopped over at Vic Anderson's store at the north end of Brightsand Lake and ran into Joe Maresty, at whose stopping place I had been memorably well fed years before on my first trip up the old "Boggy Creek" road, then the only wagon trail to Meadow Lake, which used to see so many horses and wagons bogged down.

Joe had brought some good furs in, and he regaled me with tales of those local beauties, the Pichet girls, now both happily married. He was a kind-hearted man and an honest one, but he loved a horse trade. He had with him a young horse, but it was a bag of bones and stank something awful as the result of a wicked-looking fistula on its withers. He had been ridden right to Cochin a few weeks before by Joe's son, who was using an old saddle with a broken tree, which meant that the fork bore down with all the rider's weight.

The horse, with much cajolery, Joe now tried to trade to me for my own grain-fed buckskin with his glossy coat.

"By gar, 'ees liddle bit t'in mebbe so. But is mos' fine *cheval*, my fren'. I can take yo' poor horse for trade, no? You betcha plen' please, no?"

I said, "Nothing doing," and pointed to the big scabbed-up sore, which was oozing matter on the swollen and fevered withers.

"I'll tell you what I'll do," I said, "I'll fix that fistula for you."

Joe stared. "How you do dat?"

"With a knife," I said. Joe shook his head.

"She's plenty sore, that place," he said, "she's mebbe no heal over. I try by dam' for heal him over – now you say knife? Sapree!" Joe spat.

"Okay. It's been done lots of times," I said, and turned away. Joe caught my elbow.

"Mebbe, by gar, you got somet'ing. Dat *cheval* she's look like die – so what's matter?"

"Got a real sharp knife?" I asked. "Long blade?"

He produced a six-inch narrow steel blade.

"Just the thing," I said. "Now, Joe, put a twitch on his nibs and hang on. This will hurt a bit. Wait, let's put him in Vic's single stall, so we can stop him rearing up or breaking out. And Vic, bring a couple of lengths of lamp wick, will you?"

We soon had the horse in stocks and I took off my coat. One good aim, and a thrust to the hilt of the knife, which entered eight inches below the withers to travel upward at a sharp angle. The animal grunted with pain and rolled his eyes. I withdrew the blade, and out gushed a green and yellow mass. The same on the other side, and nothing remained to do but push up the lengths of lamp wick for drainage.

You could feel the tense muscles of the horse relax, and you could sense the relief from pain which resulted.

"Okay, Joe," I said. "Wash him twice a day with a little salt and baking soda in warm water, and keep those drains open for a bit, and he'll be all right. And say, Joe, throw that damned broken saddle in Beaver River and get a good blanket from Vic here to pad the new one.

That's too good a horse to have as a cripple."

"By gar'me," said Joe, "I'm goin' get this horse fat an' trade him to somebody, for sure. W'at I owe you?"

"Not a thing, Joe – this isn't my job. Just do something for me some time, Joe."

"Mebbe catch beaver so you can pinch, eh? Not me, my fren'. An' say – w'y don't you quit this business an' settle down some nice place for w'at you call 'vet,' eh?"

I rode on to the village of Waseca. There, the dray man told me, "There was a feller in from south of Lashburn early this morning and he was looking for you. He says he had a badger trap stole out of his pasture last night. He thinks it's these Indians from Winter, down by Manito Lake. I reckon he'd like to see you. It's Bert Smith."

Bert Smith told me he had set a trap in a fresh badger hole in his pasture, in sight of the Unwin Road and separated from it by a fence. He had gone down early in the morning and found that the badger had been caught all right, but both it and the trap were gone. Tracks in the soft snow showed that it had been taken through the fence to the road. It had frozen really hard that night and the tracks were set, so the theft must have occurred the evening before. Then, Smith's neighbour to the west told him that he had seen a couple of Indian wagons going southeast. He thought they were "those Desoto Indians" going home from some do at Onion Lake.

"Those Desoto Indians" was the local name for a band of Saulteaux (Chippewas) who normally camped in the Manito Lake sand hills. They had no reserve and were not "in treaty," for a very good reason. It appears that when the treaty commissioners met the Crees at Fort Qu'Appelle in 1875, the Saulteaux questioned the commissioners overmuch and aroused their antagonism. The old chief therefore broke camp and led his little band westward to continue "living free." (Later on, the Saulteaux did sign a treaty, and moved onto a reserve at Jackfish Lake.)

I jogged on for another twenty miles, feeling sure the Indians would cross over the Eye Hill Creek near the village of Winter. As I rode into that hamlet, I saw, tied to some poplar trees behind the Chinese café, two teams of lean Indian ponies and two light wagons.

"Here they are," I said to myself, and tied Buck close by. I noticed the Indian shags were munching on oat hurdles. I entered the café and saw in the right-hand booth a big Saulteau whom I knew, with another man who was strange to me. The big fellow was Jim Gopher, a sort of subleader. He was one of the most powerful Indians I ever saw, broad of beam and large of hands, which is uncommon in a people usually so lithe and slender.

I nodded and went right past, sat down in the next booth, and ordered coffee. Before it was brought, I heard the Indians get up softly and pad out on moccasined feet.

I quickly followed. They were at the wagon, Jim lifting something out of the mess of straw and old blankets in the wagon bed. His head was down, and I had walked to his elbow when he raised it, together with a large badger, frozen hard and with a heavy steel trap still clamped to a leg.

"Jim," I said, "that badger is stolen. Give it to me."

"My badger," said Jim.

"Bert Smith's badger," said I. "You stopped your wagon at Bert's pasture and stole that lot. Put it down. You know the law, Jim. Trapping is one thing, stealing another. That badger I seize," and put out my hand.

The younger man never moved or spoke. Suddenly, Jim raised the frozen steel-shod animal right over his head with his hands. His stolid face creased savagely, his somber eyes stared into mine. He spoke softly but sibilantly – we were not two feet apart.

"I keel you," he said, with a sort of finality.

"For a badger, that's no good," I said, as steadily as I could, keeping my eyes on him. I tried to sound relaxed, but I was scared absolutely stiff. I was too close to think that my side arm would be of any use.

"For a badger, Jim," I said, "to hang by the neck – what will your wife say? A fine, perhaps, not for having a badger, but for stealing. Why were you so foolish? Did not the *moniyās* Bert also need that badger? Did he not buy that trap? And put it behind his own fence?"

I thought the hands gripped a little less tightly, the eyes shift ever so slightly – if I could only change his thoughts!

"Jim," I said softly, "was I ever hard on your people? Did I not speak for your band when someone tried to make trouble about your camping on company land? Give me the badger, Jim. It is not yours."

Big Jim slowly lowered his menacing weapon and allowed me to take it. Thirty pounds of frozen meat and metal. It would have cracked my skull like an egg.

"Come with me, Jim, to the store."

No one had seen the little seriocomic act behind the café, but, as I crossed the street carrying the animal, with Jim and his still silent companion in tow, I saw the faces of some people pressed against the window and peering between the bold lettering which announced: "Royal Café, Mark Sing, Prop.".

In the store, I found the Indian women trading, and great was their concern at seeing their leader apparently in the hands of the law.

I rang the local JP, who soon turned up. I charged Jim then and there, and he stoically paid a ten dollar fine, having just sent his friends to fetch a bag of muskrat from the wagon to sell as coverage for such a contingency. I said nothing of his threat – that was between us.

The badger and trap I sent by mail driver back to Bert Smith, his mark as he described it to me being on the trap.

This was the only occasion I was ever offered violence by an Indian. Those people, apart from petty felonies, were perhaps the least criminal minded in the West. I was sorry to see him fined, too, for they are always hard up. I must remark here that badger fur was popular then, and this animal would have fetched over sixty dollars – that was a real temptation.

R.D.S.

V

CARS AND CONFISCATION

THE DUCK HUNTING SEASON did not open until September 19, but late summer brought the usual spate of over-eager sportsmen and some local natives made a habit of having a shoot in August. Although the unmated drakes were already strong on the wing, many broods were yet in the late down stage.

It was a good season for wildfowl and I had little time for leisure. Cars were now in common use and hunters were everywhere.

I had come from Paradise Hill after visiting Mr. Imhoff's studio and admiring his paintings. His son-in-law was a keen hunter and naturalist and also a taxidermist, and my visit was useful as well as enjoyable.

Quite a few hunters from south of the river had been shooting, and I hoped that I would be able to check on some of them at Maidstone Ferry.

It was pretty dark when I drove down the steep, winding road to the crossing. The ferry was tied up on the opposite shore, where Montan, the operator, had his little home. I pushed the communicating button on my side. It would take about fifteen minutes for the ferry to cross over to me, as the river was low and sandbars necessitated a good deal of hard work.

I sat on the bank enjoying the still fall evening, with a hint of frost. The bare branches of the hoary Balm of Gilead trees formed a series of spidery arabesques against the blood-red western sky. The quiet placidity with which the water flowed belied the existence of the deeper currents which could be so dangerous. It was very quiet, and a small piece of dirt which fell into the water from the bank sounded like a heavy stone.

I heard a car's brakes squeal behind me. Then another. By the time the ferry arrived, there were three.

The silent ferry dropped its apron to grate against the mud and gravel of the approach, and Montan stepped over with his mooring rope. We drew on to the deck, but waited a bit, for we heard a fifth car approaching. This was a Ford with a fabric top. It too drove on. The ferryman threw the heavy painter rope aboard, raised the apron, adjusted the chain, and we started across, the only sound the squealing of the cable pulley and the soft lap of water against the wooden sides.

I began to check. The first two cars carried hunters dressed in the usual canvas coats and peaked caps and warmly sweatered and muffled against the cold. It's a chilly business waiting in a blind.

It was nearly dark and I got out my flashlight to check the guns and the bags and the licences of the first three cars. All was in order, and we exchanged courtesies. The man in the last car still sat at the wheel, so I introduced myself and asked for his licence.

"Oh, I know you," he muttered gruffly, as if annoyed, and produced his licence. He was a big man, oldish, and a prosperous farmer too, from about twenty miles south. I checked his bag. Two geese, seven ducks and a prairie chicken. I reached in for his double-barrelled gun with the remark, "Don't mind if I check your gun, do you? We have orders."

"I do mind," he said. "I hate officialdom – but go ahead, and don't shoot yourself."

I opened the gun – two shells in the breech.

"Look," I said, "this is why we check guns. There are too many accidents, and you should know – it's on your licence – that it's an offence to carry a loaded gun in a vehicle of any kind."

"What are you trying to do, charge me?" he asked, gruffer than ever.

"Young man, I'm an old-timer – I've hunted since I was knee-high and I always have my gun loaded. I'm the one who handles it, and I can't see it's any business of the game guardian or anyone else. Furthermore, I've never been checked by a game officer before, and I resent it."

"There's always a first time, sir," I said, "and it's not only for your protection, but for other people's. Don't think we like being snoopy – we just want to do all we can to stop accidents."

"You going to take my gun?" he asked.

"I could," I replied, "but under the circumstances I'm only going to warn you. I am sure there was no intent to break the law. But will you please be sure your gun is unloaded after this?"

I took out the shells, closed the gun and handed them both back to him.

"Okay," he said, but with a very bad grace, I thought. He was still muttering to himself when the ferry touched the south bank.

That night, I reached a small town and, having parked my car at the rear of the little hotel, I had my evening meal at about 10:30 p.m. in a Chinese café where they were used to feeding at odd hours.

The streets were dark and empty. A light shone from the window of the little corner drug store. This was kept by a keen hunter, who was also a licence issuer. I thought, old Dan's in the store. Perhaps I can look over his books, late as it is. The store had a sort of porch and I had just reached the shadow of this when the door opened and three men stepped out backwards, still talking to the proprietor.

"Okay, Dan," said one, whose voice I recognized as being that of a local farmer, "we'll pick you up about a quarter to five – like I said, the geese are feeding on the north barley field, and that'll give us time to get our pits dug before daybreak."

Another voice that I knew spoke next. "Well, good-night, Dan," it said. "See you bright and early."

I did not move. The three men turned away from me and got in a car. The druggist closed the door and put out the light. I heard him go upstairs to his quarters.

Yes, I knew that last voice. It belonged to a locally Very Important Person, a man I had checked before. It seemed to be well known that he used an unlawful automatic shotgun made in the States, but whenever I checked him he never had anything but a normal double-barrelled gun in his car. Furthermore, he didn't like being checked and said so.

As I knew of this illegal gun but could not find it, and felt sure he did not keep it at home or carry it in his car, was it possible that old Dan was his accomplice?

I made my plans. I told the night clerk to call me at five, fix me a bite and have a can of water for my car – antifreeze was not yet in vogue. He was well-trained in keeping his own counsel both with regard to travelling young ladies and government officers.

I was duly called and fed, and I slipped out the back way to fill my car. It was a frosty morning and I had to use the starting handle. As I was working away, I heard a car go west, and a thin shaft of yellow light gleamed for a moment between the buildings. That must be my party. The farmer's land lay west, and I thought I knew where that barley field was.

I wheeled out of the yard and followed, but I did not put my lights on. About half a mile before the farmer's land started was a cross-road, where I stopped and parked the car. I reckoned that if they had heard the engine coming they would think it had turned up the narrow road, where the bush would muffle the sound – I didn't want to scare them off.

True, the first precept was to *prevent* an infraction, but in this case the only way to accomplish this was to get hold of that gun and prove it had been used. I thought about this as I walked on, following the grass verge and listening intently. It all seemed rather a dirty trick, and I had not at first meant to eavesdrop, but it was bad for the cause for which I worked to have it "put over on" me too often. The public might think that I had no wish to tangle with a VIP.

"Without Fear or Favour" must mean *something*.

I stopped and listened at the corner of the field, and blessed the Cummings Company, which put out those clever little maps showing who owned what land. I was making no mistake – very soon I could hear the dull thud of spades from beyond the bluff which loomed darkly against the faint light of dawn. I walked on, every nerve tense. I felt grateful to the night clerk for the coffee and eggs, for it was cold.

Then, on the grass verge, a large car. Carefully, I tried the door. It was not locked. I opened it silently and felt for the car key; it was in the switch and in another second it was in my pocket. The escape route was closed.

I went silently under the barbed wire fence and crawled like a snake through the bluff. I would have to *see* the offence. About a hundred yards south of the bluff I could dimly see men putting straw and stubble over the freshly turned earth and getting into the pits.

The sky lightened rapidly until I could see the painted decoys set out in the stubble beyond the men, who now ducked their heads and were no longer visible. A mouse scuttled over the dry grass and peered into my face where I lay. It sounded like a man walking in that still hour, and my heart sounded like a drum.

So time stood still, while the blush in the east strengthened, and then I heard the geese. Their clangour came nearer and nearer, they circled, stooped and came in just over the decoys. Then all hell broke loose as five men stood up in their pits – "Bang! Bang!" Then a rapid fire of "Bangs" – the automatic.

Birds fell, some with such a thud that later their breasts could be seen burst open. They were big honkers – the prize of all winged game. The firing ceased, the remaining birds wheeled and were gone, and for a second all was quiet. Then the men erupted from their pits, leaving their smoking guns. I saw my VIP leave the centre pit and, by the time I reached it, unnoticed in the melee, the man had gathered their game and clubbed the wounded. In a glance, I took in the arsenal at the centre pit – the old double-barrelled shotgun which I had seen before and a beautiful job of an automatic, chased and inlaid on the stock with the woodwork gleaming in the sun's early rays.

The five men gathered before me, nervous, tense.

I said, "Good morning, gentlemen. A good shoot."

The VIP reached in the pit for his gun, but I forestalled him, "Let's see," I said, "you are Mr. X? Do you know who owns this gun?"

"No," he grunted.

"It is, of course, an illegal weapon and is under seizure. This is your pit, and the gun is warm. Do you have anything to say, sir?"

"Yes," he said reluctantly. "It's my gun and I don't want to lose it. It cost me four hundred dollars in American money. Can't we fix this up somehow?"

My reply was: "We don't fix things – you must know that. Now, let's see your licences."

My VIP had a licence and the farmer did not need one on his own land. Of the other three – all town men – only one was licenced. The other two, one of whom was the druggist (and licence seller!) said they just hadn't gotten around to getting theirs (although the season had been open for a month!).

Then I counted the game. Five geese was the limit and five times five is twenty-five; they had twenty-seven.

My VIP had some sporting blood. "Look," he said, "I fired the most shots, and I reckon those extra birds are mine, so don't blame the others."

I accepted this.

The birds, decoys and men all piled into the one car, with me sitting on one fellow's knees. At my corner, I had them stop and we transferred the stuff to my old Chevy. I suggested that we go into town and get some breakfast – they looked pinched (no pun intended).

Later that day, they appeared in court. The two unlicenced men got the usual fine and their guns were returned. I suggested later that the druggist lose his appointment as a licence issuer, and this was done. The VIP was fined pretty stiffly for the illegal weapon, which was not returned, and he received a small fine for exceeding the bag limit. The geese were sent to the local Red Cross hospital as a treat for the patients.

Nothing came of the VIP's threat, made in anger, of having me fired, and I did not mention at the trial that he had offered me a drink from his flask while I was on duty.

The next morning in Battleford, I opened the daily paper and saw the headline "Fatal Accident in the Community." What followed was an account of how a farmer, returning from a hunting trip, accidentally shot his wife, who was working at the stove. Apparently, when he came in, he was very cold, which may have made him careless, and as he hung up his gun on its accustomed nail the firearm discharged, and the shots went through the partition, striking his wife in the head. Death was instantaneous.

He was the man whose loaded gun I had *not* seized at the ferry a few days before.

The use of cars by hunters was the worst possible thing for upland game. Both prairie chickens and ruffed grouse love to dust themselves and feed on scattered grain along the roads and trails. "Town" hunters were the chief offenders in the matter of driving slowly along and potting these birds with .22 rifles, picking them off one by one.

On one occasion before the season opened, I heard small-calibre rifle shots ahead of me on a bush road. Rounding a corner, I saw the dust of a car ahead, but not the car. At the next cross-road, I could not determine which way the car had turned.

I turned in to a farmhouse nearby to see whether they could help me. When I knocked at the door, a voice said, "Come in!" The farmer's wife was just drawing two prairie chickens, over which she hastily drew a sheet of newspaper. She flushed and faced me. I pretended I hadn't seen the birds and asked for her husband.

"He's at the barn," she said.

said, "Oh, I know what you're after – tough luck! Y'know, with the harvest on, I just don't get time to go to town, and a fellow has to have some meat! What'll it cost me?"

I thought quickly. I knew this man didn't take a tenth of the game the sportsmen did.

"I don't know what you mean," I said, "and I'm in an awful hurry. I'm after a fellow's been shooting from a car. Did you see which way he went?"

Taking his cue, the farmer said, "Fellow just passed going north – what – ?"

I was already driving out of the yard, and I left him staring.

I caught up with the other fellow, too!

R.D.Symons.

VI

WOMEN FOLK AND WINTER TRAILS

BUCK WAS GETTING AGED and had lost a good deal of his old fire. He suffered from rheumatism, and I concluded that for the winter's work I had better purchase a new second mount – tramping through the winter snowdrifts ages a horse.

I thought of Phail Murphy, a genial old-time rancher who ran his horses along the breaks of the Battle River near the Little Pine Reserve. On my next patrol, I turned into his yard.

Phail was breaking a horse to harness. He used a most ingenious device for this. In the centre of a round corral was a stout set post. From this, about three and a half feet up, a strong pole extended at right angles. This pole had a circular steel band at the big end, which encircled the pole, set in a deep groove. The other end was axled into a single wagon wheel. To the outside end a pair of birch shafts were hinged at right angles to the pole, behind which was a single tree. To the pole itself, just behind the shafts, was bolted a metal implement seat.

Phail would harness a colt, get it into the shafts, pick up the lines and vault into the seat. No matter whether the colt went straight up, ahead or backwards it could not get away and had to go in a circle, and Phail could urge it ahead with a whip or stop it with the bit.

On this occasion, the colt was brought to a stop, and Phail met me with an Irish grin. The colt started up.

"That's okay," said Phail, "I let him run sometimes. He'll just go in a circle, and he'll be learning." He had tied the colt's head with a lariat to a hook at the top of the centre post to keep him from lunging outwards.

We smoked and I told him my trouble, but Phail shook his head. "Any saddle stock I have," he said, "is either too old, too light or too young for your purpose. I'll have to go out of horses soon, anyways. I'm getting on, and so much land is being taken up that the range is getting scarce. But the worst thing is we daren't burn the range now – and gosh! Just look at the brush!"

We looked. From the river breaks across the valley to Blue Hill and beyond seemed almost all white poplar except for the higher sand ridges.

"Yes," he went on, "when I came here forty years ago this was practically all open prairie and the best grazing you ever saw. Now, there's precious little feed in that heavy poplar. Pity."

I agreed, and rode on to George McLean's near Carruthers. George was another old-timer from Eastern Canada, a man of great resource and earnest rectitude. Later he was elected to the legislature.

He had come west in the nineties, first as a school teacher on the Blackfoot Reserve, but he was a pioneer type and had made a wagon trip from Battleford westerly "into the blue" in those days when the only railway was the main line; and, here, in the lovely Eagle Hills, he had started his ranch of both cattle and horses.

But George had no horses to spare. We had a good visit and George showed me his two new shorthorn bulls. He had some calves to "alter" and I lent a hand. (In fact, I was often asked by farmers to alter their calves. As an ex-rangeman I was quick and expert, and helping people always led to better relations – as one man said, "I think more of a game officer who isn't afraid of a little cowshit on his breeches.")

As I was leaving, George said, "How about Ed Southwick up by Lashburn? He's had a real good stud for years now, and I bet he's got a colt would suit you. His mares are mustangs, but that stud's a thoroughbred, and big. Give him a try. You stay here over night – it's pretty late – and you can get to Ed's early noon tomorrow."

So the next morning, I struck out. The days were getting shorter, with a hint of snow. I was glad of my angora chaps and buckskin coat, but by mid-morning I had the coat tied behind the saddle, for I wore a heavy sweater beneath it.

Southwick's place had been described to me as "a big white house and a big red barn above the river breaks," and about noon there it was. I rode in by the big gate, dismounted and knocked at the door.

Mrs. Southwick came to the door. I announced myself and asked for "the boss."

"He's at the barn," she said, pointing.

I led Billy over to the big sixty-foot barn with its hip-roofed loft.

Mr. Southwick was feeding a team, but he put down the hay fork and came to meet me.

"Ain't you the game warden?" he asked.

I admitted I was.

"Yes," he went on, "I knew you by your hoss. I raised him as a colt and sold him to Nelson at Battleford, and he told me he'd sold it to the game warden. Well, what can I do for you?"

I told him.

"Well, young fellow," he said, "I've got two or three colts you could pick from. Fours and fives and maybe a six-year-old. You'll have to break him yourself. I'm asking a hundred and seventy-five each. But say, it's 'most dinner time, so put your hoss in and I'll slip to the house and tell the Missus you'll be here to dinner. I'm as hungry as a coyote, and we can go through the colts after. They're down the pasture about a mile – 'long the river."

He went to the house, and I followed him after unsaddling Billy and feeding him hay.

Mrs. Southwick indicated the washbowl and towel, and I noticed the table was not set in the kitchen, as is usual on a weekday for farm folk.

They led the way to the dining room, complete with Congoleum rug, heavy furniture, lace curtains and big oval photographs of an older generation. Beneath one was a black coffin-plate bearing a name and the words "Mother at rest."

Evidently, I was "company."

The meal was delicious but conversation was stilted. Southwick was not a talking man, although a very good eating one. Mrs. Southwick asked a few polite questions. I knew her at once for a type which, while the salt of the earth, was just so narrow that they seem to see sin in all around them. The kind that mentions certain animals by such deceptive names as "gentlemen cows" and "big horses," and then only when mention is unavoidable. I felt sure she kept away from the barnyard, and would not even venture there for the hen's eggs.

"May I smoke, Mrs. Southwick?" I asked in my best company tones.

"Indeed you may not!" she replied. "*None* of my family has ever contaminated themselves with tobacco. Besides, it smokes up the curtains."

(I thought Mr. Southwick choked, but he recovered quickly.)

"And furthermore, young man," she went on, "I hope you do not carry spirituous liquors with you. *None* of my family even knows the taste of rum. My father and my grandfather devoted themselves to the cause of temperance, and fought vice and sin to their lives' end."

She looked at me severely. She was a handsome woman, and her white hair gleamed like silver. I assured her I did not carry any rum with me, and added I was sure her parents were to be congratulated. Could I, however, smoke on the porch?

She bowed gracious consent, and I sat on the porch steps with my smoke.

Presently, Mr. Southwick came out. "Let's go see them colts."

We went to the barn and saddled our horses. He said, "Before we go I must show you the sire of them colts!"

He led me to a gloomy area in the back of the barn where, in a roomy box stall, a fine stallion whinnied softly.

Mr. Southwick let down the bar and we entered. He told me the horse's pedigree with some pride. I patted the animal's neck and talked to him.

Mr. Southwick had disappeared. "Hello?" I called.

"Coming up!" was the reply.

As I turned, I saw my host, just rising from his knees in the far corner. In one hand, he held a bottle, in the other a plug of chewing tobacco.

He came across the straw to me. He pulled the cork from the bottle, took a good swig, passed the palm of his hand over the bottle's neck to render it sanitary, and held it towards me.

"Don't be afraid of it, young feller," he said. "It's White Horse – best in the West."

I took a swig, complied with the sanitary precautions, and passed it back. He took another swig and offered the bottle again.

"Enough for me, thanks," said I.

"Okay," said he. "Have a chaw?"

"I'd rather smoke," I said, "but I'll wait till we get outside."

He held a finger to his nose. "Beware of fire," he said, "hell or otherwise, eh?"

He replaced his booty in a hollowed-out log. We mounted and he steered me across a field to the pasture gate. Not a word was said.

At the gate, being the younger, I dismounted and held the barbed wire-and-post contraption to one side for him. As he rode by, he checked his horse slightly and, stooping over the saddle horn, he spoke huskily in my ear. "Young feller – remember – what the wimmin folk don't know, don't hurt 'em."

With a sly wink he clucked to his horse. We looked over the colts and I chose one. We made a deal right there, and I got the animal for a hundred and fifty dollars – perhaps he forgot that he had said a hundred and seventy-five, or perhaps the whiskey had mellowed him.

As I said goodbye, I could not forbear one question.

"Mr. Southwick," I said, "what about the smell when you go in the house?"

He grinned. "Oh, that? Horse medicine!"

It snowed that night, and next morning I started across the rolling sand hills heading eastward. I intended to check up on a young Metis I'd been told was shooting muskrat along the river in defiance of the ordinances prohibiting the taking of these animals in the fall.

I hit a prairie trail which led from the village of Bresaylor (named after three old families – Bremer, Sayers and Taylor) to the Battle River. Albert lived with his mother and married sister just off the trail about a quarter of a mile from the river bank.

I didn't relish my task too much, for times were pretty hard by now and work was not easy to get, and anyway I had a lot of sympathy for the native people – but I hadn't made the laws, and Metis had the same status and responsibilities as other people. I have paid more than one small fine for such people myself, and furthermore I often pleaded their difficulties to municipal authorities and assisted them in obtaining relief.

I like the Metis – so cheerful, so hospitable, ready to share the last pinch of tea or bannock with you. So polite they are, too.

There was not a sign of a track on the fresh snow. No dog greeted me in the little clearing, but smoke plumed from the stove pipe. I knocked and heard the usual "Entrez!" I was quite aware they had seen me coming, through a chink in the logs.

The married sister, carrying a child, opened the door and I stepped in. Albert's mother, a stout and smiling woman, sat on a large nail keg with some needlework in her hands.

"Bo' jo', m'sieu," she said courteously, and , "Bo' jo', madame," I replied. We plunged into the Lingua Franca.

"Mebbe you look for mon fils?" the stout lady went on.

"Oh, oui," I replied. "It's Alber'que je voule talk wit'. Dey tell me he's set dose trap for wutchusk, a bord de la rivière, non?"

"Non, m'sieu."

"Mebbe he is using paskissikum? His twenty-two fusil?"

"Non, m'sieu."

"Dey say he's catch plenty dose rats, mak' le bon chasse?"

"Non, m'sieu."

"You know, naturallement, madame, de law he's say you don' catch dose rats en l'été sauvage – in the Fall time?"

"We know, m'sieu. Nous savons bien."

"I guess I got to take a look." I sounded serious.

"Comme vous voulez, m'sieu." A shrug of those enormous shoulders and a lugubrious simper.

I searched the simple cabin. I found nothing.

"Where your boy – Alber'?" I asked.

"I guess he go wit' team. He go to Bresaylor – I don' know, me."

"No track," I said.

"I don' know, me." Again that shrug, as if a she-elephant were dislodging a rider.

"Your pardon, madame," I ventured, "ayez le bonté – if you please to rise from where you sit – take another seat?"

I was suspicious of that nail keg.

"Certainment, m'sieu." Madame rose in huge dignity. As she rose she pressed her hands to her lower thighs, as if for assistance, but as she walked over to the bench she held them there, and the tell-tale crackle of rat skins (which sound like crumpling paper) told me there was no need to look in the keg. She sat down slowly, with dignity, like a duchess, I thought. The younger woman busied herself at the stove, shifting the kettle noisily. The child said something, and was hushed.

It was very quiet. I looked sternly at the old woman and she heavily at me. Then the corners of her eyes crinkled and her mouth widened and, in another second or so, we were both laughing till the tears streamed down our cheeks.

"Madame," I said, when I could control myself, "you are a very naughty woman – très méchant femme. Is it then you use dose bloomers for a cache? Shame on you."

She had the grace to blush – a blush that showed through the tawny smoothness of her cheeks.

She knew and I knew that I could go no further. The police matron was at North Battleford, seventy horse-miles away.

I left, but as a parting shot I said, "You better watch those rats – they'll be needed to pay Albert's fine when I catch him!"

I rode on up river. No tracks. I reckoned Albert must have a tent somewhere. In another mile, I caught a gleam of something in a thick willow grove. Tracks led from it, but not to it.

It was Albert's tent all right. I found some rats on stretchers and another five unskinned. It was a mild day and they filled the tent with their sweet, musky odour. I made a cigarette. Presently, I heard a crackle and two dogs bounded through the willows followed by Albert, a .22 rifle in one hand and a bag of rats in the other. He had no time to dodge.

I escorted him to Maidstone and he was fined ten dollars for taking rats out of season. I did not add the charge of using a rifle, which was forbidden then on account of the number of wounded rats which were not salvaged. However, few got away from the native people.

The JP said, "I know the game guardian has warned you several times. I'm sorry to see you here, for I knew your father, and he was a good man."

Albert replied, "I don' want to come. It's dis man bring me!"

We had to confiscate the rats, but the JP gave Albert orders for twelve cords of wood, which would bring in even more money, and he was allowed two weeks to pay his fine. As for the rats in the bloomers, they no doubt helped too.

I could not forbear sending a box of sweets to Albert's mother – she was an admirable woman and deserved them!

Snaring of coyotes was prohibited. Not only was it a cruel and horrible death for the animal, but snares were often left on the cowpaths all summer, and anyone who has ever seen a horse limping along with its hoof rotting and a cable-wire snare right to the bone around the fetlock must support the ban. Many farmers and all rangers agreed that the law was a good one, and its enforcement was pressed.

I had made a patrol to Manito Lake and found a few snares, also one poor barely alive coyote, its throat almost cut, its teeth broken and its gums bleeding from its desperate attempts to bite its way to freedom, which I put out of its misery. I could not pin the perpetrator this time – that had to wait for another year.

However, on my return to Battleford, I found a letter from a rancher at Sonningdale (about forty miles southeast) telling me that when he rounded up his horses he found one dragging a snare. He had been obliged to shoot the horse, as the hoof was about to drop off, but he had sawed off the leg and saved it for my inspection. He had his suspicions, and would tell me more if I would try to get out to see him. He had no telephone, but that was something I used as little as possible, as there was a lot of "listening in" on rural lines. You would ring a number and take down the receiver, and then you would hear "click, click, click" as one by one other receivers were taken down and everyone was ready to hear the latest gossip.

It was early in January and about thirty below (Fahrenheit) when I set out. I was not able to leave until nearly 11:00 a.m. as I had a lot of reports to get off, so I had lunch before I left. I kept my horse in the livery barn and the barn man asked, "Which way you goin'?"

I didn't usually say, but this time I told him. "The Old Saskatoon Trail."

He shook his head. "Don't think that trail's been broke out this winter – not this side of Baljennie. Mostly they go across the river to Denholm."

"Oh, I can make it, I guess," I replied, and mounted. The barn man was still shaking his head.

We trotted down the smooth trail and across the bridge. Sure enough, when we turned left under the railway trestle the old trail did not show a single track. That railway is the one that eventually came up from Biggar – it was never much of a show, for it crosses a couple of Indian Reserves which didn't require much in the way of freight or passenger service.

The snow was deep and crusted, and Monte (my new horse) was soon slowed to a steady walk. I already had him gentled down and hardened up, but he felt his oats and plunged impatiently through drifts for the first hour at that racking half trot which throws a horse up and down as he pulls his legs from the snow, a gait which every rider knows and hates. One can only stand in the stirrups like a cameleer and bear it as best one may.

But five miles of that changed his mind, and he slowed to a steady plod, his hooves breaking the crust noisily. This was a lonely road; for the first fifteen miles only two holdings adjoined it, and now both houses were empty. One family had moved out and the bachelor who used to live in the other was dead.

Monte wanted to turn in at the buildings, but only halfheartedly. Even he seemed to perceive that vacant aspect of the untrodden yards and the frost-closed eyes of the small windows.

We called this the "Old Saskatoon Trail," for the other end, finally lost in a network of roads where the hills flattened far to the south, could once be followed to Saskatoon. But there the name became the "Old Battleford Trail," for it was up this trail that the Barr colonists had urged their oxen, horses and wagons from the Temperance Colony to Lloydminster.

Many were the axle trees which fell apart on the narrow, gullied track, with its ravines and sharp turns and always the steep hills to the south and the river to the north.

Some of the settlers near Baljennie first started up this route, but, seeing lush meadows and grassy lands, had halted their gaunt cattle and fallen-to with axe and saw, content to rear their log homes where the fancy pleased them; content, too, that the rest of the column should push on into further hardships. One of those to stay was Arthur Bater.

There was no wind and little sign of life. A few rabbit tracks padded between the willows and the slots of a deer crossed the road and disappeared up the slope, zig-zagging through the greenish-grey blur of poplar boles. Once I heard a soft note and, looking, I saw a group of pine grosbeaks in smokey grey alight in the brush to pick daintily at some late cranberries, led by a red-washed male.

It was getting colder. My horse and I were hoary with frost and we both had icicles on our noses and mouths. I stopped to breathe Monte and took off my mitts for a quick smoke, but my fingers were clumsy and Monte's heaving sides made them clumsier and paper and tobacco floated to the snow.

"Come on," I said, and my voice sounded far away. We plodded on. The dusk thickened – the sun sets early at that season. Monte's breath around us, the somber brush slipping by so slowly, the creak of leather, the muffled "brunch-brunch" of hooves – in this I lived small, wizened, a speck of dust in a frozen cosmos. If only the road were good. It is not hard to keep warm at a trot, but this plug-plug was different.

I peered ahead for the first light I could expect – twenty miles out.

I was probably making three miles an hour, but perhaps less. It would be about 5:00 p.m. – the sun set at four. Bater's ranch *must* be near.

I was cold. Even the three pairs of socks and the good moosehide moccasins, even the buffalo coat, the heavy mitts, the woolly chaps and the muskrat cap – none of these were enough against the biting frost. Br-r-r-r-r – it must be forty below, and my face felt stiff.

I dismounted slowly, stiffly, and felt my feet break through the frost. I stood gripped to the knees, as was Monte. He clicked his bit and rubbed his nose on my chest to dislodge the icicles from his lip, and the rough push almost knocked me down.

"Come on," I said, and slowly got ahead of him. Tramp, tramp – Monte stepping in my tracks. A moon was coming up. Not more than a hundred yards could I make. A snow-covered log made a bump by the trail side. I sat down, my legs trembling. I saw the same flutter in Monte's shoulder muscles and I thought it was like a poplar leaf in the evening breeze.

I felt sleepy and my head swam. But something said, "Don't sit – get on with you!" It took me what seemed hours to mount. The walk had warmed my feet but, although I brought Monte up to the side of the log, I found that even with that advantage my arms would hardly draw me up; but I finally mounted and urged Monte on.

I was in a semidaze, cold beyond shivering, when Monte raised his head with a jerk that brought me to. With a mittened hand I clawed the ice from my lashes. There, to the right, was a dim square of yellow light. Bater's ranch!

Then I thought – the gate! For the buildings were three hundred yards off the road, and I well knew there was a gate where the trail turned off. If that gate was closed, as it usually was, how was I to get off and open it? And if I did could I make it to the house? For I knew I could not remount.

Suddenly the muffled hoofbeat changed to a sharp, staccato squeak. I was on a good sleigh road, and opposite the buildings. I did not need to turn Monte's head to the right. Like a homing pigeon he swung toward the gate, his keen instinct sensing a warm barn. (In such intense cold there is no scent – not even from a barn yard.)

And now for the gate. Monte did not pause and I realized we were through it. By a lucky chance it was open. The square of light became larger. The big log house loomed up. Monte was by the window on the right of the door. I could look in. I could see the warm glow of the wood heater. I could see Mr. Bater, slippered and snug, reading his paper, Mrs.

Bater knitting and the youngsters deep in their homework at the table.

I had no voice and I felt that what I saw was far removed from me, but I managed to urge Monte a few feet and then with my moccasined foot I thumped the porch door as hard as I could.

Country people have ears for sound. Every noise means something to people who are alert to a horse kicking in the barn or a dog scratching to be let in. Their ears are not dulled as are those of city folk who are subjected to all the sounds of traffic, of slamming doors, of whining refrigerators or bubbling steam pipes.

I heard Mr. Bater's voice. "Jack, there's someone at the door," and a shrill voice replying, "Aw, dad, you're always hearing something." Then Mrs. Bater saying, "Your father's right – go and see what it is."

The door opened and there stood Jack, a well-grown youth, just looking.

His father brushed past him. "It's the game guardian, mother," he said, as he pulled me like a child from the saddle, calling over his shoulder, "Jack, put Mr. Symons's horse in."

My heavy outside clothes were torn from me. Hot tea found its way like a blessing to my inner parts. In fifteen minutes, I was tackling a hot meal, and then, relaxed and smoking, I answered the questions which my kind host had patiently kept back.

When that was over, Mr. Bater looked up over his pipe and said dryly, "It's only fifty-two below zero – what's the matter, you getting soft?"

The patrol was successful, but it took three days of plugging through deep snow, three days of following tracks in the steep, heavily wooded hills, before I finally ran down the man I was after. One of the things he said ruefully was that he didn't think anyone would bother him in that weather!

Thirty years later I revisited the scene. The Bater house still stood and the son operated the place, but now a car road a little to the west of the old narrow trail took one to Battleford, and the hills looked smaller and less formidable.

A copy of my report is before me. It reads:

Jan. 5, 1931: Patrol 12:05 p.m. to Bater Ranch, Baljennie.
Re: Complaint snaring S.E. Baljennie.
Supper and bed Bater ranch.
Road bad, snow deep, 52 below p.m.
Miles 20, saddle.

Jan. 6, 1931: Patrol 9:30 a.m. Swan Lake and Cooper Creek.
Supper and bed Bater ranch.
Snow deep – few trails broken.
Miles 21, saddle.

Jan. 7, 1931: Patrol J. D'Arcy's farm 10 a.m.
Found snare signs near south boundary Keppel forest.
Supper and bed, J. D'Arcy.
Still cold, 43 below.
Miles 22, saddle.

Jan. 8, 1931: Patrol from D'Arcy farm 7:30 a.m. in direction
yesterday's signs. Still dark and struck fresh horse trac
Finally apprehended A.B. of C. taking coyote from sn;
Patrol p.m. to Lizard Lake with prisoner.
Court at 4 p.m. Convicted – so much and costs.
Record of conviction, etc. follows.
Still cold 35 to 45 from noon to late p.m.
Miles 16, saddle.

Jan. 9, 1931: Patrol from Lizard Lake to Thompson Ranch.
Noon at Thompson Ranch.
Patrol 1 p m to Battleford with seizure (7 coyote pelts
Arrived Battleford 7 p.m. Packaged pelts for shipment
Regina and forwarded conviction reports and my costs
attending court $2.
Road good by Red Pheasant – only 19 below.
Miles 32, saddle.
Total miles this patrol, 111.

VII

CHANGES AND CHASES

THE YEAR 1932 BROUGHT many changes. In that year, the old Department of the Interior at Ottawa gave up control of forests, lands and fisheries, transferring these resources to the western provinces from which they had been withheld.

We all wondered what our fate would be in the sorting out which followed the formation of the Saskatchewan Department of Natural Resources. The older employees of the Department of the Interior were retired on pension and the pick of the remaining were retained, and the best of the provincial game officers were amalgamated with them to form the new department. I was among these.

Each game officer (the title was now field officer, Department of Natural Resources) thereafter had the full responsibility for all these resources in his district, and these districts were cut down to more workable size. I retained about two-thirds of mine, including the string of lakes north of Battleford – including Jackfish and Murray – which were the great commercial whitefish lakes of that time.

About then, too, an RCMP subdivision was set up at North Battleford. Inspector Spriggs was in charge. He was a good friend of mine and in times of stress he was always ready to spare me a constable to assist. In turn, I helped them when called on with my intimate knowledge of the people and the country, which often came in useful. It was the happiest possible association and I look back with satisfaction at the patrols on which I accompanied Sergeant Chalf (Raddison), Corporal Fielder (Lloydminster), Corporal MacRae (North Battleford) and many others.

It was a Sunday in the late summer. I had visited the village of Cochin and now stood on the bridge which spanned the creek connecting Jackfish and Murray lakes. Idly, I watched the weekenders from the city as they fished or rowed their boats under the bridge. Motor cars were not the ordinary man's transport, and that great "summer resort" industry, which now stalks everywhere, was just beginning to yawn and stretch.

My attention was caught by a rowboat coming towards the bridge. Its occupants intrigued me. A handsome young Metis rowed the boat skillfully, and opposite him in the stern sat a pretty blonde girl, while in the bow a greyhaired man sat smoking. There was a strong resemblance between the older man and the girl.

There was nothing extraordinary about this. The Metis, of whom there were many in the Cochin area, often rented boats to holiday makers, and as often rowed them and guided them to angling ground – but I knew all the Metis boys for miles around and this one was strange to me.

Then, just as they passed under the bridge, I heard the girl say to the young man: "It's time to be going home – father's getting tired."

I wondered whether they were married, and where her mother was.

That evening, a man I knew well came to me and said, "Some guy has stolen my net, and gosh! I need it. If it wasn't for that domestic licence I'd have a hell of a job to feed my family."

"Tell me about it," I said. "Where was it?"

"Set just outside the swamp, on the Murray Lake end of the creek. I set it Saturday night and went to lift it Sunday morning before too many anglers got going – you know how they raise hell with a net! Well, it was gone – I mean, it wasn't just bashed into or anything, but just plumb gone. I couldn't locate you before. I've been asking everyone, but I guess I'm out of luck unless you can help me. Is there anything you can do?"

"Not much right now," I replied. "If it's theft, it's really a Mountie job, but I'm going to North Battleford, so give me all the particulars you have and I'll tell them about it."

He described the net, an unusual thirty-yard gillnet of five-and-a-half-inch mesh with his card and licence number (27) tied to the guy pole. Both poles were gone too, and the card, of course. He had no suspicions and had seen no strangers. I made no comment.

Sharp on Monday, I was at the police office. Corporal MacRae was helpful, but he said, "Well, we've got an awful lot of work and we're short-handed. There's so little to go on, too." He stubbed out his cigarette and added, "Say, you know the country and you know fishermen – couldn't you investigate?"

"Certainly," I said, "as long as you say so."

I told him about the strangers and he looked up some files. "Well," he said after a bit, "we don't seem to have any record of a young white girl married to a Metis – that is, not of the ages you say. But keep in touch, and call us if we can help you."

I left. I already had a rough plan of action. First, I visited all the secondhand stores. I asked if anyone had tried to sell a net, as I thought it just possible that someone had take it for a couple of dollars of quick money, but I drew a complete blank. Of course, it had been Sunday, and that cut down the chances.

Then I called on the filling stations. At about the fourth, which was at the south end of the town on the road to Battleford – Number Four Highway to Swift Current – the attendant said he had served a dark young chap driving an old Model A pickup. He said he looked like a Metis, but he was not a local boy, and he had noticed a pretty girl friend with blonde hair – yes, there was an old chap half asleep in the back. This had been late Saturday night. The man had paid him and then they had driven north. He had not seen them since. This implied that my party was from the south, probably some distance south, or they would not have needed gas on their way up.

I went the round of the restaurants. At the Club Café, I found that three persons answering my description had come in for coffee, and had asked for lunches to be made up, at about eleven Sunday night, and the waitress thought they might have been fishing because they were laughing and talking about "the lake."

So I started off south. If on their way they had asked for lunches, they must have had quite a drive before them. They had quite evidently crossed the bridge, so I followed Number Four and didn't even stop at Battleford, as it looked as if they had done their shopping. They wouldn't be on the Indian reserves, so I went on to Cando, where I didn't get a clue – they would have passed there after midnight. I went on to Phippen, as I knew an old-timer there who was well acquainted for miles around.

I drove into his yard, where he was fixing some machinery.

"Hello, young feller," he said, "what's on your mind today?"

"I want to rob your brains," I answered.

"Okay, shoot." He sat down on the disc and bit off a chew.

I asked what Metis, if any lived down around those parts (I didn't know of any).

He thought for a while. "Well, some of the Trottiers could be around, picking rocks and so on," he said.

I shook my head. "I know the Trottier boys."

I changed my tactics. "Do you know," I asked, "is there a widower man around here who has a nice-looking daughter and may have lost his wife in the last few years?"

"Well, let me think…." He looked across the flat prairie and chewed. "Let's see now," he said after a bit, "there's old Frazer – no, that won't do. Lost his wife in '31, but he moved down Saskatoon way and his kids were growed up."

"Wait!" He slapped his thigh. "There's Ben Taylor – is it Ben? – no – wait a bit – Ed. That's his name, Ed Taylor, used to live over west on the school section. His wife, she died of TB down at the San a couple or three years ago. *He* has a gal – only one in the family. Little bit of a white-haired thing 'bout fourteen she were. Yep, old Ed Taylor and his gal. He was cut up some and sold his quarter. He was a kind of a good guy. Don't just know where he went, but I did hear – was it Biggar? or Kerrobert? – Somewheres that-a-way. Sorry, I can't give you more facts."

I thanked my friend and pulled out for Biggar, where I went to the municipal office. I knew the secretary and asked him if a man called Ed Taylor had farmed in that municipality, near the north end, if so, would he give me his address?

I soon had my information. The secretary turned from the big table and said, "Here's your man – Edwin James Taylor. Northwest Quarter, Section A, Township B, West of the Third Meridian. Sold out in 1930 to George Underdahl. George ain't finished paying for that land yet, so he should have Taylor's address. I'll give him a ring."

A few minutes later, I had the information I wanted penciled on a scrap of paper: Ed Taylor, General Delivery, Springwater, Saskatchewan.

I headed for Springwater, half an hour's drove away. About two miles from there, my Chevy needed some water, so, when I saw a man working on the land near a farmhouse, I stopped, crawled through the fence and waited until he came my way. He shut off his tractor and I asked him if I could get water at his well.

"Sure, you can," he said. "Take a drink while you're at it. It's the only sweet water hereabouts – most of its alkali. Why, people come from all over to fill their cans. Gets to be a nuisance sometimes, but a feller has to share it. My cows got out once and a little old fellow from 'way back was here for a can of water and he drove them outa the crop afore they bloated – so, you see, neighbouring pays!"

"Would that be Ed Taylor, by any chance?" I asked on a hunch.

"Why, sure that's the old guy's name – you any kin to him?"

I said, "No, I'm not, and I'm not a collector either!"

As I hoped, the farmer was both curious and garrulous. "This Ed's a queer old fellow. He told me only last week he wanted to go up north somewhere to catch some feesh. Now me, I hate feesh – I'm from Iowa and give me pork! But, anyways, he seemed set on it. Why in tarnation anybody would want to go 'way up there in all that heat and dust for a few measley feesh?"

"Oh, he must have a car, then?" I ventured.

"No, he don't, but his son-in-law what's married to his gal, he's got an old pickup. Rattly old thing. I reckon he must've gone too, and the gal. They got no kids – yit."

"I wonder," I began, "how the old man feels about his son-in-law. Some of those old-fashioned fellows might think their daughter's too good for a Metis?"

"Not old Ed, I reckon," replied my informant. "Ed ain't much good himself since his wife died, and when Johnny Langlois came to help with the harvest and fell for the girl, Ed sees his chance for a hired man – free; and that was that."

While telling me this story, the farmer had waved his hand vaguely to the south. I hadn't wanted to ask him directly where the old man lived, so I turned south on the first trail, which ended in a correction line, but a little-used prairie trail wound off to the southeast and I followed the twin ruts for about half a mile and then, between two low hills, I came to an untidy shack. An oldish man was digging a mess of potatoes for his dinner. As soon as I got up to him I recognized him.

I asked where his son-in-law was.

He waved toward the continuing trail. "'Bout half a mile," he said, "by the big slough on the other quarter. What do you want?"

I told him.

He looked me up and down. "Now, look here," he said, "I don't know nothin' about no net – wouldn't know one if you had it in your hand. Sure, I fish when I get a chance – I use a rod and line or a troll. I got me two pike and a pickerel Sunday, but I don't know nothin' about no net."

I said I would look around. I did. No net, only a couple of pike heads on the slop pile, buzzing with flies. I started down the trail again. I could see a big grove of willows and, beyond, the gleam of water. I drove on and saw no house, but a tent. A typical Metis summer camp, I thought.

The young woman was hanging some clothes on a line. She flushed and put her hair back as I left the car. I told her who I was, and said that I wanted to talk to her husband.

"Johnny's gone over west with a load of poles," she said. "We're fencing this quarter. We just bought it from the CPR."

"Well," I said, "I'm looking for a net – a stolen net, Mrs. Langlois. You don't mind if I look around?"

"Go ahead," she said, but her voice was very small. I felt a beast.

It wouldn't be in the tent. The truck was gone – with the posts, I supposed. The willows looked the best bet and I threshed through them. Their coolness was pleasant after the heat of the bald-headed prairie and there, laid out to dry all of sixty miles from any lake in an open spot among the willow bushes, was a thirty-yard five-and-a-half-inch mesh gillnet. I realized it had been kept under or in gunny sacks until they got home and was now drying out so as not to mildew. A good job, too; this man knew nets. The floats were neatly laid out and the lead weights aligned with precision.

Just then, I heard the rattle of a light truck. It stopped. I heard voices, and then the young man parted the willows and faced me.

"What's the idea?" His brows were black.

"The idea," I said, "is that you are under arrest. I charge you with stealing a gillnet from Murray Lake early Sunday morning."

"Not me, Mister," he snapped. "I'm not a thief. I never saw this net – I never saw it before."

"Are you trying to tell me," I said, "that someone laid this net out here, fifty yards from your tent, without your knowledge?"

"I don't know how it came here, and I don't care how it came here. If you want it, take it – I wouldn't even know how to use it!"

"You won't deny," I went on, "that you *were* at Murray Lake – at Cochin – on Sunday, with your wife and your father-in-law?"

"How do you know that?" he replied. "What makes you so smart?"

"Well," I laughed, "I get so smart because I stood on the bridge and saw you and the others in the boat, and," I added, "you drive a Model A Ford pickup and your name is Johnny Langlois and your father-in-law's name is Ed Taylor, and you put in six gallons of gas at the B.A. Station at North Battleford, and on your way back you had coffee and bought a lunch at the Club Café, and your father-in-law caught two pike and one pickerel, and you took that net up just outside the swamp where that little creek flows into the lake again, *and* you have been a net fisherman – had enough?" I stopped.

"Okay," he said. "I took the net, but I still wouldn't know how to use it. I figured I might sell it. Anyways, they always said they couldn't fish with a net in summer, so the fellow had no right setting it, is the way I figured. Stores were closed in North Battleford, so I had to bring it on here."

"Well," I said, "just roll it up, will you?"

I turned away, but as I turned I noticed how meticulously he rolled it, clinking weight to weight and float to float. To the uninitiated, rolling a net is not easy. He was positively deft.

"And you said you knew nothing about nets!" I said when we reached the car.

He flushed.

So he was taken back to Battleford and paid his fine. The net was returned to its owner and the case was neatly tied up – as neatly tied as any case Sherlock Holmes ever put his pipe to!

When I was down in that country a year or so later, I called in, for I felt that the young woman had a tough row to hoe and I wondered how they were getting on.

The old man had died, the farm was prospering, the young woman had a baby and Johnny was working hard.

Over a cup of tea, the girl said to me, "You know, that net business really straightened Johnny up!"

It really was a successful hunch I had about that net!

That fall, I had much to do. The hunters were active after ducks and geese and I made many trips keeping poachers off the Saskatchewan River game reserve, which extended along both banks from Prince Albert to the Alberta boundary.

Geese, while feeding morning and evening on stubble, must have fresh water near their roosting places, and the river sand bars are their favourite roosts. So long as geese are not shot in such places, they will stay until late in the Fall, but a raid on a sand bar or a rifle shot from the shore will send them clean away – so the only way to get good goose shooting is by protecting the river banks.

The fresh water marsh at the south end of Big Manito Lake was another such spot.

On one of my patrols, I dropped in at the ranger station at Yonker one Saturday. Jack Sufferin, who took care of the provincial forest, was a man of mixed blood married to an Indian woman. There was not a woman in the land to exceed Mrs. Sufferin for courtesy, kindness or hospitality. She could set a tea table which might have graced a London home, and had a ready laugh when amused.

I spent that day patrolling the sand hills and enjoying the many little white-beach lakes. I had the Chevy and got stuck in the sand once or twice, but I knew the remedy for that – a big strong tarpaulin laid down – and I soon got out.

At Dilberry Lake, I met a party of shooters from Provost on the Alberta side. The evening was cool, and they gathered around a fire to warm up and make coffee. One young fellow started to unload his pump-gun and it went off just between two fat businessmen. No harm was done, but the young fellow looked quickly at me with a very red face.

I went back to Jack's for supper, and he asked me if I could stay over Sunday. He said there had been quite a bit of shooting over by Reflex Lake the Sunday before – fellows from Alberta, he thought – and perhaps we could make a joint patrol. A pinch or two, he suggested, would stop this Sunday shooting. I agreed, and we started off next day in Jack's old Forestry pickup with grub and tea pails to make a meal.

It was one of those delightful days we get in September. The colours were blue and gold, blue of water and sky and gold of poplars just turning – those crooked little sand hill poplars with their bleached white trunks, their black feet showing they had once been licked by a thin grass fire. The sun was hot and there was so little wind that even the poplar leaves were still, or almost so.

We had a good lunch – trust Mrs. Sufferin for that. A roast prairie chicken sandwich with fresh bread and butter and blueberry pie, all washed down with that outdoorsman's delight – strong tea.

We left the truck in a hollow and found a vantage spot on the nearby knoll. We lay down in the shade of some wolf willow and dozed. About 3:00 p.m., we heard a car coming from the Alberta direction, heard it bump and scrape through the low scrub.

"That will be hunters," said Jack, and we rose to our knees, peering out west through the purple stalks of the silvery willow. Then we saw the car, stopped and parked like ours in the shadow of a bluff. The blue lake gleamed not over two hundred yards away and we could see a mass of ducks floating on it.

"Wait till they show themselves," I said, "and until they get far enough from the car that they can't make a getaway."

We waited, and time went on – three minutes, ten minutes – they should be quite near the shore.

Then, suddenly, "All right, you guys, don't move!"

We wheeled. Two men had come up silently behind us – two men who had been stalking *us*!

One, a Mountie complete with stiff-brimmed Stetson, called out, "Don't try to get away. We saw your car and took the key. Easy, now – where are your guns?"

We got up shamefacedly. I said, "Good afternoon, Corporal. You make a pretty good poacher yourself!"

He recognized me. "Good Lord – *you*! Martin here told me there's been a bunch of Saskatchewan guys Sunday hunting along the border and fished me out for a trip. Oh, my aunt!" He collapsed with laughter.

His companion didn't see the joke and turned sulkily when I told him that, even if he was a voluntary game guardian in Alberta, he had no business in his semi-official capacity on the *Saskatchewan* side. (He was a local postmaster.)

"We are in Alberta," he said, "that's Blueberry Lake."

"*We are in Saskatchewan*," I replied, "that's Reflex Lake."

"Damn these sand hills!"

About one hour later, we picked up two real Sunday hunters from Lloydminster, so the day was not wasted, but it gave us a different point of view; we'd seen things in reverse, and it didn't feel nice. It also taught Jack not to leave his key in the truck!

I went back by way of Lloydminster. I thought I could have a try at apprehending a man I had missed several times. He was an American who had a married sister near Kitscoty, Alberta. He used to come up from Iowa driving a fast Cadillac, and for two falls now he had shot on the Saskatchewan side without the required nonresident licence. It would have to be an alien nonresident licence at that, only to be obtained by applying to a provincial game officer or at the department at Regina. I knew he only had an Alberta resident's licence, for we have our ways of knowing such things. Several times I had almost got him, but his car was too fast and I was only allowed by law seven miles close pursuit across a provincial boundary.

However, I thought I'd tackle it again and luck was with me. I found out at Hall's store in Lloydminster that the geese were feeding up Tangleflags way and I drove up there. Geese were all over the place. I parked my car behind a bluff just near a prairie trail which angled west across a school section.

I heard shooting to the east and then I saw his car – I knew it, a pale grey Cadillac sedan – coming slowly down the road. I thought, "I'll stand in the road and stop him" – if he would stop, which I doubted.

I stood behind a willow bunch in the ditch, but he turned off on the prairie trail, driving slowly and watching a skein of geese to see where they would alight. I saw my chance and sprinted for the Chevy. I had perhaps a mile and a quarter to catch him before he struck a good road to the other side. I shoved her into second, then into high, and roared after him. Two setter dogs looked at me through the rear window, and I could see the Iowa licence plate.

He increased his speed, but his car was not made for prairie trails as mine was. He nearly cracked his pan on a rock and slowed a little. Just ahead, the trail passed between two bluffs where there was only room for one car. I clung to the wheel and drew alongside him, catching him on the left side with my bumper. I had the road. His Cadillac lurched to one side with its bumper against a stout poplar.

I jumped out. The Cadillac man was livid. He half opened the door to get out and I reached in quickly and had his car keys. Then he jumped out. He was a big, florid man and he was angry, but I calmed him down, seized his car, his two dogs (he nearly cried then), his two beautiful guns, his shells and some geese and grouse (the latter now out of season). All this stuff I transferred to my car and then told him to drive to Lloydminster and not to try to get away, as I had the evidence and I could get him again with a summons. I followed close on his heels.

He swore and bluffed in court, too, and twice was warned by the JP that there was an added fine for contempt of court. It all cost him about two hundred and fifty dollars, which was light. His car, guns and dogs were returned to him and he left for home. We never saw him in Saskatchewan again.

The local hunters were well pleased; he had spoiled some of their best shoots by disturbing birds before anyone could get a shot, as his second gun was a rifle which was used to make the birds get up in the hopes that they might offer an overhead shot.

But it was time to get back to Jackfish Lake. The shore ice would soon be forming and the whitefish would start to spawn. It would be the time of the fish poacher's harvest.

VIII

REGULATIONS AND RECONNAISSANCES

WITH THE REORGANIZATION OF the department, I had become a fisheries officer as well as a game guardian, and fish – whitefish, to be exact – was to become a major part of my responsibilities. Fish poaching was running rampant, and had been for years!

The Fishery Act was clear cut: there was a complete protection of fish at spawning time, strict limits on the size of the catch, and limits on the size of gillnets to assure that young fish could escape. All of these rules, and the welter of regulations that backed them up, were designed with just one thing in mind: to protect the fish and assure that there would continue to be a resource in years to come.

And whitefish was a valuable resource. In addition to providing winter food for the natives who lived around the lakes, and many others who used fish to thicken their stewpots during those hard times, whitefish fetched twenty-eight cents a pound, sold in bulk to commercial buyers who would come up from New York and buy right on the ice when the season opened. Poachers, on the other hand, were lucky to get a nickel a pound, but did that dissuade them? Not in the least. The public, no doubt feeling the price of fish was too high, provided a ready black market; nor can you discount the pioneer spirit of adventure and free enterprise, with the spice of risk attached, that motivates many men, not to mention the prestige among one's peers earned by outwitting the law.

Up until that year, the law had proved to be all too easy to outwit, and the lakes had been all but ruined. All that was soon to change, however.

My first concern was to make myself something of an expert on whitefish. As the various lakes had different seasons, dependent on the natural spawning cycles, fish taken at one (closed) lake was often passed off as coming from another, where the season had already opened. But the fish vary considerably from lake to lake, and it didn't take me long to be able to distinguish between those caught in different waters. Being a fair hand with a pencil, I also made careful drawings (with the aid of a microscope) of the scales of whitefish – pickerel, pike and mullet – and detailed drawings of their insides; this would prove invaluable while giving evidence in court, as under the Fishery Act, any part of a fish – even so small a part as one scale that might turn up on a fellow's pants' cuff – was considered a fish. Being caught with the scale of a Jackfish Lake whitefish on your pants when Jackfish was closed was as good as a conviction.

My next task was to attend the fall meeting of the local fishermen's association, which was held in a village hall and was well attended.

Nudges and whispers and a murmur of low talk greeted me and I was under many eyes. I could feel that I was being well sized up, and I determined to be short and to the point.

I told them without preliminary what they already knew, the state of the lake. I made no bones about the reason – the lake was poached out. I said I would not waste time explaining the Fishery Act to them; they knew it better than I – especially the loopholes. I spoke in praise of the former inspector as a man and a gentleman. I reminded them of the old saying "good policeman, good SOB" and I said I was just that. I told them that just as they studied the act for loopholes, so I studied it for means of conviction.

I sketched in the laws of evidence. I told them something about fish, and that I had the means at hand to prove that such a kind of scale or set of insides belonged to such a kind of fish, and that the fisherman caught before December 15 with whitefish scales on his clothing or shoes would likely be convicted. I would show absolutely no quarter for one scale or for a ton of whitefish.

I told them that I would enforce the laws on seizure and confiscation, that a man caught on or near a lake could find himself and his vehicle searched, and that if any equipment was found he would be lucky to get off with the clothes on his back – even "Iceland mitts" were fishing equipment.

I knew, I said, that these illegal activities had tentacles stretching as far as Saskatoon, Regina and Prince Albert, and that they had spotters, spies and friends everywhere, that I was aware of their moccasin telegraph and their system of flashlight and truck horn signals, that I knew the former inspector's every move was known at all times, and that even in Saskatoon they had friends who would send word back if he stopped their overnight.

Very well, I would use their methods. I would spy – even lie, if need be. I would have my signals and would be everywhere, and if they thought I would sleep quietly in my bed on dark nights they had another think coming. I had heard threats. I had been tipped off that the lake was not a safe place for me on dark nights. I was no greenhorn. They doubtless knew something about me, and they might do well to remember that I had spent many much more dangerous and far darker nights on patrols in No Man's Land. I pointed out that this group had been asking the government to limit fishing licences to residents of the district – those living within a few miles of the lake. The government, I said, had an equal right to expect that, in asking this, the fishermen should show their good faith by doing their share in protecting the industry. They had not done so. I added that, if their attitude was a bluff, I was prepared to call it, but that I also knew many of them personally, I knew their families and their homes, and knew them to be – in all other ways – responsible and decent people. It was up to them.

I walked out in utter silence. No protestations of innocence nor promises of reformation.

The war was on. I thought I might as well start right now.

That night I rode along an old poaching trail. The night was dark and I walked my horse as noiselessly as I could. Ice was making and the ripple of the water heaved in low swells, breaking the jellified crust with a tinkling noise. A few more nights like this and shore ice would be firm enough to walk on.

My horse stopped suddenly, stumbling and threshing. I jumped off and turned on my flashlight. Two barbed wires strung across the track! I got Monte out unharmed. He was trained to wire, but if I had been at a gallop...?

Well, I thought, my fine-feathered friends, this is a start. Forewarned is forearmed. I can sneak through the brush with the best if I have to.

At the lakeshore I walked out on a rotting catwalk and again used my flashlight. The whitefish were "running." Under the rubber ice I could see them – a beautiful sight for an artist's eye, pink and gold, with jewelled eyes and waving fins. They were coming in at nature's urge to drop their orange-coloured spawn in the shallow grooves which they would make in the sandy bottom, females stout with unborn life, the smaller and narrower males prepared to cover the golden masses with the milt which would start that life growing.

I caught two men that night. I heard their boat in the black dark. I heard them get their nets to the edge of the shore ice. I followed them quietly as they left, led by the muffled sound of their oars. I found the boat among the willows and saw a bright light gleam as they entered a house at the edge of the village. They would lift that net before daylight.

I was there as they stepped ashore in the dim dawn, while the village slept on.

I had seen them in the second row at the hall the night before and I was not surprised. By 10:00 p.m. they had been tried and convicted, and their boats, their nets and the pile of silvery fish locked up in my big storage shed. This catch formed the nucleus of what would become many thousands of pounds of fish. The fish, boats, nets, sleighs and other equipment would be sold by auction when – and not before – the season opened.

I must add that the earlier inspectors often sold such seizures right after a case, and I was put under some pressure to do the same, but stood firm. To sell illegal nets now would mean they might be used again right away. To sell the fish was to give someone a "lawful excuse" to be in possession of fish out of season. It was a loophole which I blocked.

A restaurant keeper in North Battleford might buy fifty pounds of fish from a game officer and then, as fast as he sold them, replenish his stock with purchases from a poacher, being covered by the receipts he had been given by the game officer.

Within a week, the lake was frozen over, which meant it could be travelled on silently from any direction.

Jackfish and Murray lakes had a combined area of something over two townships, with up to sixty miles of shore line, most of it rugged banks slashed by timbered coulees, almost every coulee having a trail which gave access to the lake.

The greater part of Murray Lake was bordered by the Moosomin Indian Reserve, while a scattered Metis settlement faced on the northeast shore of Jackfish Lake, next to a smaller Saulteaux reserve.

The west side of Jackfish was farmed mostly by settlers of French Canadian descent, while the south sides of both lakes adjoined settlements of Anglo-Saxon and Scandinavian people.

The main road from North Battleford to Meadow Lake crossed the narrows between the two lakes at Cochin. This was the road by which a truck could go to Saskatoon or Regina, southeast toward Yorkton, or southwest to Rosetown and Swift Current. Hundreds of side roads and trails joined the main road, and the poachers and illegal truckers knew every nook and cranny of the terrain. They knew every landing place, every dim trail, every side road, fence, gate and building. Many were closely related and some were linked by telephone.

It was my task to know the country as they knew it who had tramped the hills and woods since childhood. It was up to me to know every relationship – who had a cousin or son-in-law at Saskatoon or Rabbit Lake or St. Walburg or Battleford or Rosetown. It was my task also to sort this out to see that only heads of families had permits, that only one domestic net was used, that the permit number was placed in view, and that the net did not remain in the lake between the sets which could give a family fish enough for a week or more. For when the fish ran, any old half-rotten net could fill itself several times a day.

All this took a lot of work, of course, and, in spite of my efforts, I knew that many tons of fish would be hidden in stubble, in bluffs, in hay stacks. I found opened caches, but no evidence except the tracks of a truck which were lost in a maze of tracks once the main road was reached. I determined to concentrate every effort on apprehending the truckers.

Thereafter, hardly a night but I was somewhere on or near the lakes, sometimes riding Monte or Bill, sometimes on foot, sometimes with the Model A pickup which now replaced the Chev and gave me a truckbox in which to stack seized equipment and fish.

Sometimes I went to bed and then crept out to my barn when the moon was black. I would lead my horse (saddled and with his feet wrapped with sacking so as not to allow a telltale squeak on the frozen snow) circuitously and by devious ways through farmers' fields until it was safe to mount and head off in the direction I intended to take.

Sometimes, I drove with lights on toward the west end of the lake, only to switch them off and circle back many miles to come in to the south side unnoticed. At unexpected intervals, I abruptly changed my tactics and operated by day, nearly always successfully, when the poachers thought I was taking my rest after a long night out.

Whenever I made a catch in a particular place, and after the court proceedings were over, I usually made a quick patrol back to the same place. This, too, was often successful, as the poachers went on the theory that lightning never strikes twice in the same place – but I made sure it did!

When the season opened three weeks later, I had had a dozen convictions, and thereafter for four years – by which time the bulk of the problem had been solved – this fall work went on at the same pace. I rarely got more than a few hours sleep in the twenty-four, and sometimes none, for at nine in the morning I would come in with perhaps two or three prisoners and had to get them to court and take care of the seizures, which would take until noon. Then in early afternoon, I had my report to make out, and, by the time that was finished, dusk was falling. I might doze in a chair after an early supper and be out on the lake by seven or eight. Often, many endless hours of waiting were involved, until the poachers returned to the nets they had set at dusk and which I located.

It was the hardest work I ever had to do, but I was young and active, and I loved it in its impersonal aspect, although I hated to be hard on people who had wives and families – even though it was ultimately to their own benefit.

IX

TEAMS AND TRUCKS

JUST SHORTLY BEFORE THE season opened, the moon was near the full, and with cloudless skies it was difficult to cross a lake without being seen.

I knew that two men from the French settlement were fishing all-out in a bay at the north end of Jackfish Lake. I had seen them on two nights, but they had seen me first and I could not get near them. I particularly wanted to catch them in the act.

So one night, I rode Billy up to the Saulteaux Reserve, where I called on my old friend Wabanase. I offered him two dollars for the use of one of his ponies, his old sleigh with the low hay-filled box and his old set of harness. He was amused to think of the *Kinosēwikimāw* (me) driving such an equipage, but was glad of the two dollars.

My plan was to jog across the lake on an Indian sleigh trail which came close to where these men fished. This trail ended up at a Metis house where the woman was a Saulteaux, so it was common for relatives to cross at odd times for a visit. South of this house for about a mile was a steep bank, at the end of which a (normally) sandy trail went up to an old-country Frenchman's house. This man − a very reliable and law-abiding man − had a small store, and the trail went by the store and out to a north-south road which led over the steep hills to Jackfish church and post office. This road had been graded, but the grade was narrow and the ditches deep, as the work was a local farmer's effort using horses and slushers (or slip-scraper). The men I was looking for lived south of the store, and this was the road I suspected they were using.

On this road, I knew, one could put no reliance on tracks, as the Jackfish people travelled it regularly when hauling wheat to Meota. My hope was to get close enough to these fishermen to be able to apprehend them, but I knew they used a really good team of blacks, medium-sized animals which could travel and were grain-fed − so, if a chase should develop, I wanted Billy.

I jogged slowly over the lake, hunched in a blanket among the hay and singing in an Indian sing-song, harness flapping and sleigh squeaking. Billy I had put on the off (or north) side, so that he would not be too conspicuous in relation to the worn-out, spiritless shag which was his harness mate, and I had a job to hold him back, as he wanted to keep ahead all the time.

About half a mile out, I dimly saw the big caboose and the black team. I thought it must be a cracking team, as few fishermen used a team and caboose openly like that in the closed season. I got closer and closer. The two men were lifting a net and I could hear the catch thudding into the fish boxes. One, a short stout man, looked up, apparently talking to his taller and younger companion, and they went on with their work. My ruse was so far successful.

Now I could see the team close up, and the caboose with smoke coming from its stove − Jove, they believed in comfort! In front of the caboose, which had its door in the back, was the usual plank platform which fishermen use to pile their nets and, sure enough, there was a big pile of them − if they ran all those in before midnight they'd really have a catch by dawn!

I had approached slightly angling, but now I left the twin sleigh tracks in the snow and drove straight for them. They dropped the jigger line and ran for the caboose, and I stood up and lashed the shag − he was holding Billy back when he tried to run − and was alongside by the time the men had climbed into the caboose and grabbed the lines, which ran through a hole in the front wall.

I jumped for the net shelf in an endeavour to get the lines from the outside and stop their team, which the men were urging on. WOW! I landed on the back of my head, stunned and covered with a mess of nets and gear and planks. Those damn planks! They hadn't been fastened down and when I jumped on them I had upset the lot.

My team had only gone a short way and then stopped. I ran for them, gathered the lines and jumped into the sleigh. The caboose was swaying and disappearing down the lake.

In a frenzy, I lashed that tired old horse, and cursed him horribly. No good – we were losing ground. I saw the caboose lurch up the Frenchman's trail, heard the runners squeal as they cut through the snow to the soft sand below, and with one last belch of smoke the outfit disappeared over the bank. I too reached the bank, but the shag had no more stomach. Quickly, I unhitched Billy, leaving the shag to stand with heaving flanks still hitched to neck yoke and eveners. I knew he'd stand for hours.

I gathered up the one line, seized a hame and threw myself on good Billy, who leaped to the bank at a full gallop with me low on his neck and the heel-chains on the traces flapping against his flanks.

A quarter of a mile and, where the road went north and south, I saw to the north the caboose top arise at full gallop. So – they hadn't gone toward home; they'd likely drive all night and try to throw me off somewhere.

"Come on, Billy!" I said, and I swear he gave a chuckle. In two miles we gained a good half mile; three miles – past old Esquirole's corrals – and I could hear the men shouting to the blacks. Another half mile and I was at their rear door, calling them to stand in the name of the law!

The door at the back opened and the taller young man (I knew him) threw something at me; I found later that it was a bag of fish and had it hit me I would have been spilled into the snow, but good Billy swerved and it hit him on the rump, giving him added impetus that brought me alongside the off black. I seized his foam-flecked bridle and pushed against his head with my shoulder with all my might, Billy holding me there like the good horse he was.

Another hundred yards and the team slowed up and, with another strong shove and Billy's shoulder ahead of the black's, the whole outfit came to a standstill in the ditch, the caboose at a dangerous angle and the blacks heaving and choking.

The tall fellow came out in one jump with an ice pick – a heavy thing of steel and five feet long – but I shouted, "Stand back, you idiot, look at your fire!" For, true enough, the angle and the heave had slid the hot little stove up against the plywood side of the caboose. The man calmed down and turned to fix it, and the older man advised him in French to be careful, as they didn't want a serious criminal charge for the sake of any number of fish.

I got the team turned around, tied Billy at the back of the caboose and started with my prisoners for Meota, twelve miles away. It was 3:30 a.m.

On the way, I stopped at a storekeeper's and woke him up. Sleepily, he agreed to take a team and pick up the nets, the planks and the jigger, to pull whatever nets were already set, to take care of Wabanase's horse and see that he got it back, and then to deliver the booty to Meota.

Thereafter, at least until the season opened, I had a fine pair of blacks in my stable, as well as a sleigh and caboose to add to my collection.

Trials were drawing a number of the public, but especially this one – half the fishermen in the district attended it. This was all to the good – word was getting around!

I was in North Battleford having a coffee in the Club Café, and, as I passed window on the way to the pay desk, I noticed three men walking by, one of whom was from south of Battleford and suspected of fish peddling. I looked closer and saw that each of them had a parcel with the label from the liquor store just up the street.

They crossed the intersection and all got into a good-sized but rather battered truck. As I could see the licence number, I wrote it down, and I was still watching them as they drove north towards the lakes.

It was about four in the afternoon and the late November dusk was already closing in. There was a skiff of snow – perhaps two inches – and I knew that, if these men were intent on obtaining a load of fish by unlawful barter with Indians, their fresh tracks would show up on one of the reserve trails. At that time, none of the Indians had trucks and there was little reason for any one else to visit the reserves – in fact, they would really have been trespassing.

It would probably take a few hours for the Indians to gather their fish from the hiding places and get the truck loaded, so I was in no hurry, but I showed myself as much as possible around town. I went to a cinema at six, but left quietly at half-past. I drove slowly up the

Meadow Lake road, ready to stop (or attempt to stop) the truck I'd seen or any other suspicious looking vehicle I might meet.

I took a good look at all trails leading into the first reserve, but there were only sleigh tracks. However, at the north end of Jackfish Lake, a track went in – the track of a truck.

I went past for a mile or two then turned around and came back with my lights off – when snow is on the ground, it is quite easy to drive without lights provided one knows the country and drives slowly enough. I turned off the road on to the trail, following the truck track, and from time to time I shut off the engine and listened and looked. I kept on for three miles and passed through the reserve; the truck tracks went steadily on, following the lake shore.

A little further on, I knew, was a cluster of Metis shacks; this was nearly at the Narrows and the truck must be there, for the little trail that ran from the village to these huts had shown only a few foot tracks when I passed it an hour earlier.

A clever ruse this, for no one would be likely to come to the huts by this devious route, yet the operators had a clear run of only a short distance if surprised, and then had the highway to speed upon.

How glad I was that I had gone so far to the north to find their ingress, and not taken it for granted that the truck had gone on to Meadow Lake!

I stopped the pickup in the deep shadow of a bluff and listened again. I thought I heard a voice singing and I climbed a low swell from which I thought I should see the cluster of huts on the bank above the lake – and there they were, even closer than I thought, and in the largest building a pale yellow square showed that behind the window a coal oil lamp flickered.

Again the sound of singing – Indian singing in a minor wail, "Ayee! Ayee!" – and then the sound of men apparently squabbling. I was about to step forward, for I could not see the truck, but just then the plank door was pushed open and a man lurched out. The sickly beam reflected a whiter light from the chrome on the bumper of a truck backed into the brush not fifty yards away, and the gleam of red beyond was from the eye of a horse, so there must be an Indian team or teams somewhere about. The man rummaged in the truck and returned to the building. "Comin' up!" I heard him say, and a gust of laughter followed.

"Now," I said to myself, "now, with a fresh round of drinks – now is my chance!" I stepped as lightly as I could to the truck, felt in the dashboard – good, a key! I pocketed that and climbed up the truck side.

Fish to the top – over a ton. I stepped to the door of a building and, as suddenly as I could, I kicked the door in and stood in full view.

"All right, boys," I said, "the party's over!"

A bottle fell to the floor. A new half-empty gallon of wine sat near the door with its top unscrewed; with my foot I hooked it and sent it rolling outside. One Indian, in the very act of downing a beer, sat as if frozen and made no protest when I took the bottle from him and transferred it to my pocket – since it had no cap on, most of the beer had spilled over in all moving about, but there was enough in the bottle to produce next day in court.

Two of my men made a dash for the truck. I let them go while I put the third under arrest. Two Metis and three Indians sat impassively along the wall and I called them by name and told them to come along. The two teams of ponies and the broken-down sleighs I did not put under seizure; no fish were in the sleighs and I had not seen them unloaded into the truck. Besides, the Indian Department usually applied for and got back such equipment (except nets) because the Indians were wards of the government and minors in law, so seizing the horses would simply cause a lot of trouble and delay.

Out at the truck, the two men were still grumbling, each accusing the other of having the key.

I put a stop to that and told them to get in and drive the truck till we came to my pickup. When we reached it, I took two men in the front, put the Indians in the back and told the other man to drive the truck ahead of me to North Battleford. He was to drive in second gear only and stop if I flashed my lights twice, and I stayed on his tail. Passing another Metis cabin, I asked the occupant to let the wife of one of the Indians know what was happening so that she could arrange to have the Indians' ponies taken home.

The Indians I only charged with illegal drinking and they paid their small fines cheerfully. They knew that I did not concern myself too much about the little matter of taking a drink or two and that they were really being punished for their part in the illegal fish operations.

The Metis were charged with aiding and abetting by allowing their buildings to be used. They too knew the real reason behind their fines, for, of course, they and the Indians had supplied the load of fish.

The three fish peddlers were charged with two offences: giving drinks to Indians and unlawful possession of whitefish in the closed season. To completely tie up the barter-of-liquor charge, I had gone to the liquor store and obtained the sales slips showing what each man had purchased. This, together with the half-full jug of wine and the bottle of beer I had seized, was sufficient.

They all paid their fines and were told they'd have to find their way home as the fish and the truck were now government property. I hired a man to drive the truck and contents to my yard, where the battery was removed, pending sale.

Very shortly afterwards, I had two similar cases.

In the first case, on about November 24, a large truck with two men in it stopped at the bridge by the Narrows, and I saw one of the men slip out and go through the willows to a Metis cabin. I was waiting for him when he came back.

"Where are you from?" I asked.

"Rosetown."

"Well," I said, "I'll give you a tip. Don't try to get any fish. The season's closed and it's not safe, and you were not in good company a moment ago. No doubt you know the man who lives there" – I pointed – "and we watch him pretty close. If he has offered you a load of fish, my advice is to turn around and go home."

"I don't know nothing about fish," the fellow replied rather belligerently. "I'm going north for a load of Christmas trees – up to Meadow Lake. That fellow just told me the way."

"That's fine," I said, "the highway's marked. Be sure you get your permit from the office at Meadow Lake, that's all. I may be checking up when you come back."

Next day, I phoned Meadow Lake. Had they given a permit to so-and-so from Rosetown for cutting Christmas trees? No, they hadn't.

The day after, at 2:00 a.m., I heard a big truck go by. I was staying over at the Narrows and had lain down fully dressed for half an hour and I was out to the pickup in a flash. The tail light of the labouring truck was disappearing over the hill to the south as I started the engine – I knew I could catch up on the next hill, for the load was heavy.

Catch up I did, and worried them to a stop, although they tried to keep going. They were two angry men. Sure enough, a big load of Christmas trees and no permit; that was not too serious – it was what might be underneath that interested me. I started to throw out the little evergreens while the men shouted that I'd pay for any damage.

It was quite a load – a cow moose, and underneath her about half a ton of Waterhen Lake fish.

Two weeks later, two trucks, one large and one small; again a man seen talking to a native over a cup of coffee.

I warned these men too. They were from Kerrobert out on the prairie miles away.

Yes, they knew Jackfish Lake was closed, but they were going to Waterhen. I suggested that they didn't make any stops on the Indian reserves en route.

Off they went north, but the more I thought about it the more I thought they seemed to know this area well, and it all added up to the smell of fish.

I stepped over to the phone and called George MacCaskill, the local ranger at Glaslyn fifty miles north, which they had to pass to get to Waterhen. I asked George to look out for them, gave him the licence numbers and asked him to call me about supper time if he had anything to report.

I did routine work till then, but shortly after I'd eaten at the little café, I was told there was a call for me. It was George. He said, "Listen, those trucks pulled by to Swanny's Hotel and the fellows had supper. Then the small truck went south for half an hour. It came back fifteen minutes ago and both trucks have just gone south together. Good luck!"

Again, I waited about an hour, then I pulled out and drove north and found a truck leaving the reserve. This time, I got two truck loads of fish, about a ton and a half. They protested they were Waterhen Lake fish, but I knew they hadn't been there; and those silvery Murray Lake fish, all of an even size, bore small resemblance to the larger, coarser and darker whitefish which Waterhen produced. As usual, I kept one or two of them in cold storage to produce in court as evidence.

X

DRUDGERY AND DRAMA

AN ENTRY FROM MY JOURNAL:

December fifteenth, and the season opens.

For the last few days, I have been frantically issuing licences, for, under the Fishery Act, it is the officer of the department who does this, because each commercial licence is only good for the lake to which it applies.

This involves a lot of office work and I, therefore, bought a portable typewriter, on which I hunted and pecked to record the monthly reports of licence fees and sales of equipment; and realized I was responsible for a lot of public moneys.

Now the season is open, I get a little breather, not that I am idle. There are confiscations to sell. The several tons of seized fish are soon bid up by the peddlers, who load their purchases and start off to tour the countryside. Many farmers will buy a hundred pounds or so for winter Fridays.

Bids are brisk too on nets, on jiggers and on ice picks, but the small mesh nets (illegal) are, if in good condition, sent to Regina, while the poorer ones are destroyed. Cars, trucks and teams are mostly bought back by the original owners. With a nicety of feeling, which is much to their credit, few others will bid on this equipment, scorning to take advantage of a neighbour in difficulties by purchasing his erstwhile team at a cut-rate price or by adding their bids to run the price up.

There is still patrol work to be done, but it is easier now, for the fishermen are in the open.

Nets, yardage and mesh have to be overseen. Various disputes arising out of priority fishing grounds must be settled. Both sides try to win me over, but a decision has to be made and, under the act, mine is final.

At two main points on the lake, fish buying stations have been established by the agents of the New York dealers. In order to keep track of poundage, these have to be constantly visited.

Many hours have I stood in the rough lumber fish shed, amid the cacophony of the ice-crushing machinery, into which one man throws ice blocks, while another scoops up the crystals – enough at a scoop to pack into each box in which the fish lie head and tail.

Hammers ring all night, putting together the wooden boxes, packers' helpers tear oiled paper from big rolls for a lining; the packers sort out fish for size and species from the big piles just released from the weigh-scales. The catch is not all whitefish, there will be some pike and barbot to be consumed locally, and now thrown aside. But there is also pickerel, which New York loves.

Quietly, deftly, the fish are packed, the crushed ice put around, the paper folded over, the lid nailed down. The stamp is applied with a thump – "50 lbs. Canada 'white' or 'yellow'." (Yellow means pickerel – not more than seven per cent of the catch.)

The boxes are piled by the back door. Trucks back up for loads – crash, slither, the boxes are stacked – a roar of exhaust and the truck heads for the railroad, passing its empty mates en route.

On the lake side, if you stepped out, the moon would be riding high, the lake ice stretching away to lose itself in the frost fog. Lights twinkle all over the lake – the lights of cabooses. You hear the snarl and screech of sleigh runners, muted sound of horses and men.

A caboose looms suddenly from the fog. You see the horses's frosty heads as they pass into the light from the door – the icicles hang on their noses, their harness jungles. A muffled "Whoa there!"

Horses stand puffing from the uphill pull. The squeak of feet as men bring in the catch – writhing fish, silvery fish, flapping still as they cascade to the plank floor.

The weighing. Credit slips fumbled into shirt pockets.

"How's the run?"

"Good so far. Running good size too – all two pound fish, eh?"

"Got to dock you for those Jumbos!" (These are extra big whitefish – from five to ten pounds.)

"Aw, hell... giddap you!"

The team wheels. The caboose lurches down the bank out on to the lake again, is lost in the haze.

Another team approaching, dim lit, smoke billowing bright in the moonlight.

Squeak and thump, grinding screech of iceblocks; tapping of hammers; tearing of paper; dry scratching of scoop shovel; voices: "seven white, three yellows" – "Okay! That's your load." Exhaust fumes, pencils scratching on pads. Daylight begins. The pale yellow wash grows in the eastern sky. The cold strengthens. Sun's early rays touch the lake fog with gold and pink.

Full daylight. The last caboose crunches away, horses eager for hay and oats. The ice-crusher stops, men yawn, shiver. They turn to their breakfast.

Fish run best from dusk to dawn, and all hands will put their feet up.

I return to my office. Click, click, clumsy fingers hit the keys and the paper rolls up. Figures, more figures. Catch last night, twenty thousand pounds; total catch so far, fifty-five thousand pounds. File the report. Coffee. Bacon. A smoke and now I can finally stretch out for a bit.

So I wrote at the time. I was always prone to record my thoughts.

Came the day when the limit of production was reached on the main lake, and the operations closed for the season.

It was time for a general game patrol, and I decided to head northwest towards Mont Nebo and Bellebutte. From lumber camp to lumber camp I went, attending to various matters.

Snow was deep and many deer were yarded, while moose had come down in numbers from the Thickwood Hills into the low-lying spruce and willow country. Times were hard and the operators saving every penny they could.

One day, I went looking for a notorious ex-market hunter who had started up his trade again. After a long search, my Alsatian – I had a dog now – uncovered his cache by the side of a bush road, well hidden under brush and snow. It consisted of three-quarters of a cow moose and seven unskinned deer carcasses, including does and fawns, and he was convicted of the sale of game.

Shortly afterwards, travelling along a main road, I heard shots about a quarter of a mile to my right. I left Princess in charge of the pickup and walked in through the thickets of close-grown and inter-locked alder, making for a timbered ridge which seemed to be where the hunter was.

Presently, I noticed a raven which sat croaking on a dead tamarack in the midst of a swampy "gut" I was crossing to reach the timber and two whiskey jacks went by me on silent wings. I knew I was close to the kill and a few steps further on I saw ahead something lying darkly in the snow, partly obscured by rising steam through which I could see the movements of a bent over man.

He straightened from his skinning, a big man, a well-shaven, red-faced man who promised to be choleric and domineering. We looked at each other across the steam welling upward from the open belly of a big bull moose.

I asked for his licence. Oh, he had it all right, but it was in camp. And, say! Wasn't I taking chances? Someone might mistake me for a moose.

I said that this was my job, and did *he* realize that it was printed right on the licence that it must be carried at all times when hunting and produced at the request of a game guardian?

Oh, he couldn't bother reading all the crap the government printed. I was free to check – why didn't I go to Saskatoon to a certain hardware store and they'd show me the stub? He was entitled to a moose, and he'd got it.

"That's not good enough, I'm afraid," was my reply. "The law means just what it says, and why should other hunters have to produce their licences and you be immune? I'll lend you a hand to finish dressing the meat so it won't spoil. I may have to seize it, but I'll meet you halfway in this case. I'll go to your camp and see that licence."

We soon finished the job and he started off northeast, the opposite direction from the road. If he had a camp up there, I wondered how he got in with a vehicle, which he must have, and there was no cabin that I knew of in that direction. We walked and walked – he was certainly fit – straight through deadfalls and tangles, but I noticed he kept looking back at our tracks and breaking twigs so he would know the way again.

I suppose we went three miles and it would soon be getting dusk. We both sweated. Finally, he sat down on a fallen tree, took out a handkerchief to mop his brow and started a chuckle which built itself into a roar of laughter.

He gasped and spoke. "Wait till I tell the boys about *this*! Leading a snoopy game guardian way back in the bush, walking his legs off. Oh boy, this is good! Here you are." He fumbled in a pocket of his hunting coat. "How's that? Resident big game licence, all present and correct!"

He held out the licence, enjoying himself hugely, but his face changed when I said, pocketing the licence, "Thank you. And now you are under arrest. I'll take your rifle. Thanks. The moose is under seizure, and tonight you will be charged with failing to produce a licence at the request of a game officer."

He pleaded, but I was adamant. "You said just enough," I told him, "to convince me that this is a deliberate attempt to create a situation about which you could boast to your friends. If you *do* tell the story – which I doubt – I shall now give you the opportunity of adding that it cost you fifty dollars and costs to obstruct and waste the time of a game officer in the performance of his duty."

I had just gone to bed one night in a small stopping house on the Green Lake Road, but, before I was fully asleep, I was rudely awakened by the landlord, Mr. Wentworth.

"Can you come down right away?" he asked. "There's been an accident. Fellow back in the bush has been shot. His sister's here."

I dressed hurriedly and went down. A coal oil lamp burned fitfully, and over by the heater sat a young girl dressed in mackinaw, ski pants and jacket, with a scarf over her head. She was staring at the floor, her hands restless.

"What can I do for you?" I asked as calmly as possible.

"Oh!" She lifted her head, her face white and tear-stained. "Oh, officer, my brother's dead! Back there...." She waved a hand. "Oh, it's awful! We were doing the dishes, Mother and I, and Dad was reading. We ... we heard a shot from Tony's room ... he's only nineteen. Dad rushed in and, oh...." She buried her face and sobbed.

I called Mrs. Wentworth. "Look," I said, "this girl's had it. Don't ask her any questions, but get her a cup of tea. Got any aspirins? Give her a couple and get her to bed. Who is she and how did she get here?"

Mrs. Wentworth told me her name and that she'd come on a horse, and added, "She lives with her parents and elder brother northwest of here, near Little Fish-Duck River. They're trappers and awfully hard up. Came from the south, they did, Swift Current way, after they'd been dried out. The brother had a mash on a little hussy what lives over east by Elk Ridge. That's all I know."

"Thanks," I said. "Now you'd better get a room ready for the parents. I shall probably have to bring them down here. Have something for them to eat, too. Don't worry about the bill for now, they may be broke."

I got hold of the son of the house and sent him on a horse to get to the nearest phone, which was twelve miles away, to call the police, and started off. The team was feeling good and I soon hit the crooked brush trail leading to the Fish-Duck. The only stop I made was to ask old Dionne the whereabouts of the girl's home, and in another hour I saw a gleam of sickly light and smelt pine smoke.

The parents were in a bad way, the father trying to comfort the mother. They asked if I was the police. No, I told them, I was the game guardian and that, as the police would not be able to get there for hours yet, I would take them to the stopping house. The father showed me the blood-spattered bedroom, divided from the adjoining room by a thin partition, and I saw the poor body lying half off the bed with the .22 rifle by its side and one foot with the boot and sock off – there was no doubt that it was suicide, and the toe had pulled the trigger.

"Poor lad," said the father, "his girl friend said something cruel, I think. He has always been partly crippled and she probably sneered at him. His sister knows more."

"Right now, your wife comes first," I said. "She can't stay here. I'll take you both down and the place will be cleaned up when you come back. Stay with her and leave the rest to me."

They were soon ready and I returned with them to the stopping house, where Mrs. Wentworth took charge of the unfortunate mother and tried to comfort her. The girl, quite worn out, was asleep, and the boy who had gone to phone was not yet back. I took statements from the parents as tactfully as I could. If the phone line was down, or if it stormed, the police might take some time to get there, and some disposition would have to be made of the body. The house must be cleaned up, too, for the parents had no money for a prolonged stay at the Wentworths' and must return soon, but it would be sheer inhumanity to expect them to go back to that shambles.

The local storekeeper was also the JP, so I walked across and woke him up. His wife made coffee and we sat by the kitchen stove, he in an old dressing gown, and we finally came to the conclusion that with the evidence of three people there would be no need to leave the body *in situ* and that, even if the police could not get through, the place could be put right and the body removed. The JP felt that no inquest would be necessary, just a death certificate from a doctor.

In another two hours it would be daylight, so I decided not to wait, and I headed the team back towards the Fish-Duck. As I pulled into the yard, the grey light of dawn showed a small barn behind the cabin and a corral full of hay. I went there to stable the horses, and as I opened the barn door a cow bawled. There she was, a milk cow lately freshened, tied to a stall, and in a pen close by a fine calf just stretching itself and looking ready for milk. They had not told me of this complication. I saw the cow had not been milked the night before and her udder was swollen, so I loosed the calf and let it do the job, and fed hay to Monte and Billy to the accompaniment of the little animal's gratified lip-smacking. No other stock was in the barn except some hens which clucked sleepily in the rafters. The girl must have ridden to the village on their only horse.

I went to the cabin, filling my arms with stove wood on the way. The fire was soon roaring and I busied myself with filling every available tub and kettle with snow and set it to melt.

I went into the bedroom. First, I carefully reconstructed the tragedy and put it in writing, including the exact position of the body and the rifle and the only possible angle of fire, using a tape measure for accuracy. Next I took the sheets, crumpled and stained, and the blankets and pillowslip in the same condition, and piled them all in the corner of the kitchen.

I got the body onto the bed, removed the shirt and washed the boy's upper parts. I searched for and found a clean shirt which I drew on to him. I searched again and found first a bit of surgical tape which I pressed over that tragic little round hole in the forehead, and then a tin of talcum powder with which I dusted his face, practically concealing the patch. The boy looked clean and peaceful, as if he might have died in his sleep.

The bedding and shirt I put to soak in a tubfull of cold water. I then heated up another tub and, with the aid of a big cake of soap and a scrubbing brush, I worked on the splintery spruce floor and the half-inch lumber of the partition. Perhaps a little staining was left, but I shifted the bed over and moved a calendar to cover the mark, so that there remained at least no staring reminder.

Then I rinsed the sheets over and over again, as the warm sun lit the little cabin and put to shame the oil lamp on the kitchen table. Sweat poured from me, perhaps not all due to my exertions.

The sheets were clean at last, and hanging stiff and brittle in the frosty air on a line slung between two pines which bent and soughed in the morning breeze.

I made some tea and had a smoke. Perhaps, I thought, the parents could face life here until spring.

How hard, how bitter, to move in the winter – and where could they move in these hard times? Up to now, they had been too proud to ask for relief, but relief they would now have to accept to see them through until spring muskratting.

I found Billy and Monte ready for the trail again, so I drove to Dionne's and told him that I needed his help to load the body. He seemed to hesitate, but finally came along.

We met a police constable walking in – his car was stuck in a drift a few miles back – and the three of us went into the cabin. The constable had already interviewed the parents, and he now viewed the body and took a copy of my notes as well as the twenty-two and some shells.

"I don't think an inquest is required," he said. "The doctor can view the remains in town, so the body had best be taken there. Can you arrange that?"

I said I could, and we drove to his car, which my team pulled out of the drift.

tarpaulin and lashed it with ropes.

"Come on," I said to Dionne, "you take the other end."

"No, I don't like to touch!" He made the sign of the cross. "Dis fellow, he's kill himself – bettaire you get someone else!"

I was tired and my nerves were on edge. "Look here, mon ami," I said, "you know we are told to bury the dead. We are not to ask how they died. You are a Christian? A Catholic? Shall I tell Father LeBerre that you did not do a Christian's duty?"

He fell on his knees, again making the sign of the cross.

On an impulse, I removed by hat and bowed my head.

In this silence, I thought of the poor crippled, unhappy boy... what would life have held for him?

Then, silently, we lifted him on to the sleigh.

Another incident of that long, hard winter stands out in my memory.

I was staying at a bush post office owned by an Englishman, a married man with two children.

During the night, we heard cries and a loud knocking, and we reached the door at about the same time. A woman rushed in dressed only in a nightgown and carrying a baby. Her feet were close to frozen, and my host's wife rubbed them while she gasped out her story.

Her husband had been "acting funny" for some time. All day yesterday, he had played his "one man band." He didn't put foot outside the door. She split wood, carried water, cared for the cows. She cooked a good supper.

"He no eat – say food bad, bad. I go to bed, take baby, but Mike no let li'l boy – Alexis – go to bed. Mike, he play all time, no can sleep Alexis. I go ask for Alexis – Mike he get mad, Mike he grab it ax. Mike, he say, 'To bed, you bitch – make it move or I kill!' Two more time I try. Mike allatime mad, make it swear, chop door with ax. I get out back window, come quick for neighbour.

"Ah, mebbe Mike come for kill it me. Maybe Mike kill it Alexis. Pliz, pliz, do somet'ing!"

The lady of the house comforted her. It would be all right, the men would go for Alexis. She took the woman upstairs.

As we hitched up a team, my host told me about the woman. She and her man were Lithuanians. He used to work on the "section" at Preeceville, but he got laid off and they had come up here on a homestead a mile and a half south through the bush.

A dog was howling when we saw the light that streamed from the little cabin of mud and wattle. Through the window, we saw the child half asleep in a chair, his blond hair shining against a dark blanket. The man was playing a contraption which he worked with hands, feet and mouth – a sort of conglomeration of horn, trap drums, cymbals and heaven knows what else. The din was terrible and the dog howled again, but our man was smiling up at the pole ceiling looking supremely happy, with the ax lying on the table before him.

We went in. I got the ax from him by saying we wanted to borrow it to cut down a fallen tree on the trail. He was smiling and affable when I told him we wanted music at our house.

"Sure, Meester, I come for make it music – maybe dance!"

My friend picked up the boy, Mike carried his contraption and set it in the sleigh box and, as the runners squeaked across the indigo snow, he played to the stars which twinkled above the dark spires of spruce.

At the house, he suddenly turned savage. We had to go back, he had a job to do. He must kill it wife – woman no good – food bad – bad. "Gotta have ax!"

We told him the woman had gone to town, and then got him pacified and coaxed him down into the cellar to play so we'd have room to dance!

I sat over that cellar trap all night. No danger of going to sleep on sentry duty with the clash of cymbals and tooting of horns continuing below. My host went for the police thirty miles away.

Mike recovered completely. He had always worked with a gang until he came to the woods, and loneliness and home brew had been too much for him. But all's well that end's well, and Alexis grew up to be a respected and successful teacher at the local school.

XI

SPRING FISHING AND SPAWNING STATIONS

THE CLOSED SEASON FOR pike, pickerel, perch and other coarse fish was in the spring, the time of their running.

While there was not nearly as much work in connection with this season as in the fall, it was still necessary to keep an eye on the situation. Shooting, spearing and netting were all illegal, as were the use of night lights or explosives. George MacDonald, the fishery supervisor at Regina, usually circularized his men at this time suggesting that we should know the chief streams for spawning, and adding instructions to patrol with energy.

One cool spring day found me in the Meeting Lake country. I was on my trusty Billy and I had checked over a good many creeks, warning off some boys and putting linen notices on trees to "show willing." A farmer complained to me that his fence had been cut and that two or three wagons had gone through the night before. He said they must have been trying to avoid being seen on the main road. I took a look at the situation and decided by the direction of the tracks that they must be heading up toward Wichikan Lake; I knew that several creeks ran into that lake from the southeast and that the run of pike would be in full swing.

I also thought that, since the tracks came from the south, the owners of the wagons were probably from the vicinity of the Moon Hills. Near these hills was a large settlement of Eastern Europeans, and these people had been in the habit of netting and spearing in the spring for the purpose of using the fish for pig feed.

I had lunch with the farmer and then started out. The tracks of three wagons were easy to follow through some woods north of his land and then angling over to take one of the many Indian trails to Wichikan.

It was lucky I had a horse, for the mud was deep and the trail treacherous and boggy. The swampy wood resounded with the croaking of frogs, while in the willows the early white crowned sparrows wheezed their little songs and juncos scratched up the leaves.

Dusk was falling, but we continued to plod, Billy sometimes throwing his head as the scent of moose reached him. He hated his tail, heavy with mud, which lashed his hocks so clammily.

By the time we had covered fifteen miles, it was dark. Against the cloudy sky, the tops of the trees could not be seen, the birds were quiet and the frogs still clamoured. The damp air, so redolent of swelling buds and rotting leaves, chilled me, and I checked Billy to put on my moosehide coat and roll a cigarette. The match flared and I saw the boles of the big rough-barked poplars all etched with crisscross hatching.

We plodded on for another few miles. No need to look for the track – no wagon could leave the narrow aisle which wound through the forest. Then Billy threw up his head and snorted. I listened. I thought I heard a horse stamp and swing his trace chains.

Quickly, I dismounted. Billy started to nicker, but I put my hand over his muzzle. I tied him to some willows just off the trail, took his nose bag from behind the saddle and put a few handfuls of oats into it and slipped it over his head. A horse can hardly talk with that on.

With my flashlight in hand I walked forward as softly as I could. I could hear the roar of a creek ahead – a creek swollen to three times its normal size by the runoff from the hills. I stumbled into pools and tripped over fallen trees, but I wanted no light – yet.

A horse stamped almost beside me and blew softly, another shifted his harness and I heard the heel chains scratching on brush.

"Steady, boys," I said softly, and I reached out my hand. The warmth of a horse's body – but what part? I groped. A strap. I followed it with my fingers and found the heavy tug ring. I knew his head was to my left. I groped again and found the halter shank. Good. I slipped under their heads – I had no wish to be kicked at in the dark!

The sky was lighter now. Dimly, I saw the tree tops. Dimly, I saw I was in a small clearing by the creek. Fifty yards from me, a few red embers still smouldered from an evening meal.

I circled to the left. Two more teams and then three wagons. I listened intently. I heard voices down the creek to the right. Then a moving light twinkled, only to be hidden by a spruce. Then two more lights. Footsteps – blundering, splashing footsteps – and louder voices.

Quickly, I reached the first wagon, felt for and removed the draw bolt and lowered the eveners quietly to the leaf mould. On to the second wagon, then the third. Three heavy draw bolts. I looked around and saw three birch trees close by, three birches from one root – this would do. I hid the bolts between the roots and scratched leaves over them. I waited close to the fire, beyond which was a tent, my flashlight in my hand.

A blur of half-seen figures – I knew not how many – talking Russian or Serbian and with heavy, squelchy bags on backs. Two went right past me and dumped their bags in the wagons. I flashed my light, stepped up, and told them to stand still. Three men stood, but the others headed for the horses which I could hear threshing about in the dark. The three looked at each other and then at me. I sensed they could make off, or even attack me – two of them had fish spears.

I bluffed. "Okay, George!" I cried, waving to an imaginary companion back in the darkness. "Keep them covered!" The teamsters had their horses now and I heard them putting up the neck yokes.

"Okay, you men," I said, waving my torch, "drop those fish spears and step back." They did. I advanced and stood on the spears.

"Watch them, George!" I said, and turned to the wagons. I heard curses and yells of rage. The horses could not pull the wagons without eveners, and eveners would not operate without bolts. I told them so, and told them to leave their horses and come forward. They did. There were seven, all told. I asked each one his name. They were hard to spell, but I got them down all but two – they refused to say who they were.

"It doesn't matter, boys," I said, "you'll tell in court."

I told them to strike the tent and load it. While they did so, I situation in hand now, for no man on his feet could touch me when I straddled Billy.

I told them where their draw bolts were. I made them hitch up and climb into their wagons – two men to each of two wagons and three men to the third – and then directed them to start back down the trail ahead of me. So we plugged all night along that same bush road. The dawn began to break and the birds to cheep. A pair of mallards whistled overhead, cutting the air with a sound like tearing paper.

The light grew and I saw I had lost two men – the ones who had refused to give their names. They must have slipped quietly from the wagons during the gloomy pre-dawn hours.

On we went and it was midmorning when we got to the little town with its muddy street and false-fronted buildings.

I took them to breakfast, and by noon the five men had been fined (very lightly, for times were hard) and on their way home. I seized only the fish, about five hundred pounds of jackfish – far too good to feed to pigs!

The Fishery Act states that equipment unlawfully used *shall* be confiscated, but I had no wish to see these men lose teams and wagons, which they needed for farming, over such an offence. I got around this by failing to mention the horses and wagons in my report. I felt the two dollar apiece fine, the inconvenience and the loss of the fish was sufficient.

In the case of whitefish, I was not so lenient, of course, for the teams and trucks used in these cases were used *principally* for illegal activities, and those activities were on a more serious scale and had worse effects.

After lunch, I started out after my two escapees. I left Billy in the livery barn and rented an old car, for from here south toward Radisson the roads were fair. I soon passed the wagons of my breakfast guests.

I sped southeast until I reckoned I was exactly south of the bush we had passed through early that morning. I passed a country school house as the children were leaving, trudging home in all directions with their red lunch pails swinging. The teacher waved to them from the porch and turned back – no doubt to correct lessons.

I left the car and entered. She looked up from the desk and I asked her if she had seen two men walking down the road that morning. She said no, but one of her pupils had said that their mother had given breakfast to some men who told her they had lost their horses in the bush. They had said they lived at Redberry Lake.

I thanked her and drove on another twenty miles. It was mere routine work after that to sift out the possibles, and I shortly had my two men in the car.

After they had appeared in court, I reminded them that I had *told* them where they would give their names! They were goodnatured fellows, though, and bore little malice.

This otherwise trifling episode cost me a full night's rest plus over a hundred miles by saddle and sixty by car, but it was worth it to maintain the good repute of the department, for upon that rested the whole success of our conservation measures.

Juveniles sometimes posed a problem. We had a Juvenile Court judge (a kindly grey-haired woman), but I rarely took young people there. Usually I took whatever guns and traps they had and conducted them to their parents and had a showdown, which resulted in Dad dealing out what punishment he thought necessary and confiscating the youngsters' stuff himself.

On one occasion, I caught three pretty big boys snaring pike in the spring sun. They were under a bridge which displayed a large Fishery Branch notice of warning to the public. I saw that this was a case for stricter measures and hailed them into Juvenile Court.

They all pleaded guilty.

The judge asked whether the officer would explain the implications of the offence, and I did so.

She then lectured the boys, explaining that the mother fish must have their young ones or all the fish would die out. She concluded by saying they were naughty boys and she was fining them a dollar each, hoping it would be a lesson. They left.

I closed the court, and as I crossed the street the boys were walking down the sidewalk with serious faces and fingers upheld, peering over imaginary glasses, and saying to each other, "The little mummy fish must have their babies! Oh, fie! You *are* a naughty little boy!"

XII

DEFIANCE AND DANGER

ONE FALL WE HAD an early snow six weeks before the big game season opened. I was on patrol in the Thickwood Hill country.

Noon found me eating a solitary lunch on one of the big timber ridges from which I would be able to hear shots should any nimrods try to take advantage of the good tracking which the snow promised. Sure enough, about midafternoon, I heard a regular fusillade about three miles away in the vicinity of another ridge to the north, and set out to investigate. I followed a rough bush trail until I reached the main road. To my surprise, there were no tracks to be seen, and the thought came to me that the hunters – whoever they were – must have come in from the northeast and, perhaps feeling they might be under observation from my ridge, had made a long detour to put a higher stretch of the other ridge between us.

A very rough, steep wagon trail went over the north ridge and, not for the first time, I wished I had a horse instead of a car – on horseback

I could have been over that ridge before the poachers could dress or load their game. However, the department was beginning to think that horse travel was out of date. The police had about given up horses, too, and I knew how people took advantage of the fact that the law now followed the road.

I chided myself that I had done the obvious thing in watching from a ridge which, being of an open nature, was a favourite hunting ground – one should always do the unexpected, and I hadn't, so now I had to make a long detour and probably give them time to get well away.

I hurried as fast as the frozen ruts would permit, but that wasn't very fast. There was an east-west road about nine miles north and I hoped I might at least see or meet their truck (I felt sure they had a truck, not a car), but when I got to the crossroads a fresh track coming from the west turned north. I followed and wondered where the dickens they were going – this trail went on for miles and few people lived up there.

However, after two or three miles, the truck left the road. It went a short distance east and turned south into the road which led to the little town I felt they might have come from originally. Clever fellows, I thought – I'd give a lot to know who you are!

By now, it was dark, and when I got to the town I went straight to the café, for I was both cold and hungry. I knew the man who kept the livery barn there, and I knew he had a name as a poacher and also that he owned a light truck. I decided I would check on him as soon as I had eaten.

Halfway through my meal in a back booth, I heard three men enter with a great clomping of boots. They sat down and ordered steaks. They talked as they ate and seemed to be in a jovial mood, their talk punctuated by gusts of laughter. I heard the nasal voice of the barn man (Henry). "Thought I'd die a-laffin'" he was saying, "when I saw you miss that 'ere buck and him jest at yer elber! Ha! Ha! Bet you had buck-fever!" I pricked up my ears. "Then," the man went on, "by cripes, you hit him clean on the run, when I wouldn't have even shot!"

"Yep," another voice said, "but that was just a fluke, as you might say. The next one popped up in a sure enough hurry and I thought *you'd* missed him till he went all-over-teakettle. Say, Ed, what made *you* so slow? I didn't think you'd every get your gun up! Scared or sumpin'?"

Another laugh, and a third voice. "Oh, maybe. I didn't feel safe – those shots sure rumbled 'round the hills, and someone said that game guardian might be around."

This remark, rather timidly delivered, was greeted with a stamp and a roar of laughter. Finally the barn man spoke. "The game warden, eh? Hell, that little feller's too slow to catch a cold. Spends too much time preachin' to th' kids. I can keep tab on *him* all right. Effen he wuz around, he'll be away hell-bent north by now. I know the country better than he does. Bet you he's lost. Ha! Ha! Don't fret, the law don't scare me none. Why, I remember one time on the train to Prince Albert, I was a-tellin' one of the train crew about the time I got them beaver up to Mont Nebo. There was a old feller in the smoking room sitting quiet and lookin' us over. After a bit, he spoke up. 'You know who *I* am?' he says, 'I'm the chief game guardian and I've heard what you wuz a-sayin'. Who are you?' he says. I says, 'Me? Why, I'm the biggest liar west of the Shell River!' Ha! Ha! Them guys don't know nuthin'!"

At this point, I left my seat and walked to their booth. The liveryman's jaw fell, showing his yellow teeth. He bent his head and attacked his steak with careful concentration.

"Mister," I said, "I was just on my way to search your premises. I followed you up this afternoon. You boys can finish eating and then I want you to come with me. You are all under arrest, so don't start anything."

"Who are you?" asked the youngest of the trio, a fair-haired young man with a pleasant, but shy, face.

"I'm the game guardian you heard about," I replied, "*not* the biggest liar west of the Shell River. Now, if you please, I'd like your names, addresses and occupations."

I got out my notebook and jotted down two names; Henry's I already knew.

The younger man lived in this town and so did his companion. They were both elevator men (grain buyers) and both had come that fall from points south on the open prairie.

All denied they had been hunting – Henry vehemently and oath-fully, the other two rather diffidently. It was easy to see that Henry was the instigator of the hunt.

They finished eating and I said, "Follow me and keep together."

I led out towards the big barn on the edge of town. Henry tried to edge me around the east side of the barn, but I said, "This way," and went around the west. It had not been a silent walk by any means, for Henry protested loudly the whole way, but none of them tried to make off. It was the invariable thing that when protesting innocence such people would try to engage me in talk, all the while unobtrusively trying to edge me away from places they didn't want me to go.

It was really dark now and I played my flashlight beam back and forth as we proceeded, trying to shut out of my mind the whining voice which tried to distract me. Soon the light shone on a battered truck snugged against the barn wall, which I investigated. A pickup Ford – I wrote down the licence number. It had recently been in the bush, for willow sticks still hung from splits in the battered fender and snow still clung in frozen lumps on axles and springs. In the back were two blood-stained horse blankets; I picked off a tuft of deer hair and put it in an envelope.

The trio was silent now, just standing and watching. I announced that the truck and its contents were under seizure. Henry started to explain that he'd been out rabbit shooting. He'd got a few, and thrown them in the back – hence the fur. I didn't bother to remind him that deer hair does not look like rabbit.

I wondered where the deer were. They wouldn't be in the main part of the barn, obviously – the horses' warm breath would soon spoil the meat. They must be in the high cool barn loft, with plenty of hay for concealment, but that too would spoil them if piled before the carcasses cooled properly.

"Let's go up," I said, and started up the narrow ladder.

The deer were there, all right, not yet skinned, only gutted – two bucks and a doe hanging from a crossbeam. I made the men carry them down – one each – and load them in the truck. We drove around to the house of the local justice of the peace, who, luckily, was at home.

The charges were duly laid and the court opened. I took the youngest elevator man first. He pleaded guilty.

"Have you anything to say?" asked the JP.

"No, sir."

"Yes... Mr. Symons?"

I stated the case briefly, pointing out that the livery man knew the area well and had done a lot of hunting and was familiar with the regulations. I explained that this young man was a stranger from the prairies where there was no deer hunting and that it was perfectly natural for him to be thrilled at finding himself in a big game area and to be keen for a hunt.

I felt that he had been persuaded into this expeditions and that while, from his own words in the restaurant, he knew that the season was not open yet, he had still been led to believe that old story that "no one pays any attention to that crap up in here."

This man was fined the minimum – fifty dollars.

I then put up the other elevator man. He also, true to his salt, had nothing to say and was assessed the minimum.

Now it was the livery man's turn. He too pleaded guilty, but had a good dealt to say about snooping game wardens and the unfairness of the law, coupled with a good deal of rough language which brought a warning.

The JP then read him a little lecture, pointing out that, as a resident of the area, he was much to blame, especially as he liked to hunt and knew the woods and should be one of the first to assist in the preservation of game. He then fined the fellow seventy-five dollars and costs, which was lenient enough.

The livery man produced a fat roll of bills and slowly, like a bridge player displaying his hand, counted some out on the table. "Ten, twenty, fifty, seventy *and* five," he said, and added, "Plenty more where these came from, mister!" He glared at the JP.

"Good," said his worship blandly. "Just lay down another ten dollars for contempt of court. Thank you. Please clear the court, officer."

The venison was sent to the Salvation Army and the hides (after I had done the skinning) to the Indian department to be given to some of the southern Indians who were hard-put for moccasin leather.

A week later, most of the snow had thawed and a hard frost set in. I had just cleaned up a case of buying fall muskrats (which I found hidden in a bin of wheat) when I again found myself in the Eagle Hills.

I was riding Monte, but the brush – hazel brush – was thick, and the coulee I was descending was icy and slippery, so I was leading him by the reins. I was nearly in the open when we heard a loud "Bang!" and Monte plunged as the bullet ricocheted from a poplar trunk. I drew my side arm – a .45 Smith and Wesson – and fired twice in the air. Then I got to my feet. The man was in the open now.

"Take it easy!" I shouted, and made sure the man saw me. I went back and got Monte's reins. He was unhurt but snorting.

I approached the deer hunter and recognized him. "What's the matter, Fred?" I asked. "Got buck fever, or what?"

"Hell, no," said Fred, "but what's the idea of you snooping through the bush in a buckskin coat?"

"*And* on a black horse," I replied. "The idea is that you are only allowed to shoot bucks, and that means you are supposed to look for antlers and not pull the trigger on anything that moved in the bush! I know you never saw me – so watch yourself or I'll be having you up in court for shooting a cow moose, or maybe a man. If I had the power, I'd revoke your licence! I've had trouble with you before and if you *had* hit me, the law *might* just suspect that you did it on purpose. By the way, this is fenced land, so unless you have the permission of the owner you'd better make yourself scarce!" I happened to know the owner and that he had not given anyone permission to hunt.

At that, the fellow left in a rather bad humour.

It was only two weeks later that I had heard Fred had been killed running coyotes. It seems his saddle horse was shod in front – a dangerous practice in hill country. His hounds took after a coyote and his horse was galloping all out when it hit an icy sidehill. The horse's front feet gripped but its hind feet kept going, so it went over backwards heavily. Poor Fred was badly crushed in ribs and pelvis and died before his companions could get him to hospital.

He was a harum-scarum, happy-go-lucky sort of young fellow with plenty of nerve and know-how. It was a pity he was not in the army, where his talents would have been appreciated – in action, if not in barracks.

During these years, my interest in natural history, especially in regard to birds, never flagged. I still carried my paints, paper and notebooks, and to this day I have many sketches made while eating a solitary lunch on some patrol. Two of these in particular mean a lot to me.

One is of a pair of Bonaparte gulls at their nest in a swamp north of Jackfish Lake. What a thrill that was – the first recorded nest in Saskatchewan of these lovely, graceful birds, more like terns than gulls, with a delicacy of build and carriage altogether entrancing. I wrote to my boss, Fred Bradshaw, about them but he could not believe me and wrote back to say they must be the commoner Franklin gulls, which also wear black hoods. I finally proved my point, but that necessitated shooting a bird and taking an egg, which today is in the Provincial Museum. I was not happy about that, although there was a colony of several pairs.

This sketch takes me back to those happy days and it talks to me in bird language, bringing back the notes which resounded as I painted through the tule reeds and bullrushes, the silver bog willow and the sedges. Blackbirds and warblers and swamp sparrows were all around. Yellowthroats peered from the tangles and phalaropes circled daintily in the shallow pools, their little bodies riding high like tiny sailboats.

Another sketch on my wall is of my good Billy, saddled, browsing on saskatoon leaves above the steep banks of the North Saskatchewan. These wooded banks are shown in deep chrome and russet brown, for it was September. The smattering of spruce on the slopes is like spires among the yellow poplar leaves and the sky and water are fairest blue.

Hardly had this sketch dried, hardly had I finished my bread and cheese, ere I heard a fusillade of shots from the big sandbar island which lay a few miles downstream beyond the ferry. I heard the honking of disturbed geese as Billy and I wound down a steep coulee. The ferryman's second boat was not there, I saw, and in his yard was a big black car.

The ferryman was embarrassed and unhappy. He was a good chap – a Metis like so many of his calling – and I knew him well. Those who had taken his boat were, he said, *very* important people – something to do with the government, he thought. They had asked for his boat and he had let them have it. He had not dared to refuse. No, he had not known what they wanted to shoot. The sign, which read GAME RESERVE in black and orange, was plain to see at the ferry approach.

I put Billy in the ferryman's barn and fed him and then walked down to the boat landing. Time went on, and the sun began to sink low in the west, when another fusillade of shots came from downstream. Darkness came and still no hunters.

All that night I waited there, walking back and forth on the sandy shore to keep warm. I toyed with the idea of taking the other boat and going to the island, but rejected it. If they heard me coming, they might slip to the nearest shore and work their way to the car without my seeing. Better to stay where I was, near the car they had to come back to.

The September night was chilly. Occasionally a fish broke the water's still surface and the little rings would wink twice and then subside. Coyotes lamented from the rugged hillsides and a horned owl perched on the cable derrick hooting to his own echoes from the far bank.

I was cold and I was tired when daylight began to come. I sat down, almost yielding to the heaviness of my eyelids. Then "Bang! Bang! Bang!" and the air above me was full of honking geese. Their forms against the primrose sky and their deep cries finally faded away up the valley.

Full daylight now and the morning shoot must be over, I thought, and then I heard the sound of oars. Within fifteen minutes, I had my party lined up for questioning and had taken their guns and their geese.

They *were* very important people, who should have known better; people who thought their position in society left them free to ignore the law and spoil the shooting for others. They were not natives of my district, I am thankful to say.

They tried every argument from persuasion to bribery, from drinks to threats.

It was too important a case for a country JP, so I charged them before a rather embarrassed stipendiary magistrate, who convicted them.

Recently, since my retirement, I am told this game reserve has been abandoned as such because, I was informed, it was "not possible to enforce the law against hunting."

I wonder why?

Rumours occasionally circulated that I had been shot or injured by poachers, all completely untrue. I sometimes made long patrols, camping in the bush, so that on occasion I was not seen for long intervals and these stories would circulate.

On one occasion, someone wrote to my superior at Regina that I had been waylaid and "beaten up." Regina wired the North Battleford RCMP, who wired back, saying, "Don't worry about Symons – he always turns up."

All this seems a sad reflection on the innate decency of the people of northwestern Saskatchewan, but in the main they respected the law and, if one of our men had been injured, any one of the hunters and poachers would willingly have given aid. Certainly, we heard of occasions when officers of the U.S. wildlife service had actually been murdered in the deep South; but that was in a country known for lawlessness, a country where the federal arm was resisted with deep hatred by the professional plume hunters who roamed the gloomy cypress swamps – a people very different from our settlers and native trappers. I have been threatened and on occasion attacked, however.

Once, a man operating an illegal fish trap on the Battle River came for me with an axe. On another occasion, a wolf hunter operating illegally held me off from his shack by potting at me with a Winchester. In the first case, I was able to disarm the fellow. In the second, I had to get assistance, but that man proved to be a mental case.

Perhaps the most serious case of resistance and obstruction I experienced occurred at the mouth of a river tributary to the Saskatchewan.

Netting across a river's mouth is forbidden, and I had many complaints regarding netting for goldeyes at this spot. The culprits always seemed to know where I was, so this time I adopted a ruse. I drove boldly to a town seventy-five miles away, where I knew there lived a man who was hand-in-glove with the poachers. I registered at the hotel and went up town to eat, making sure that this fellow saw me, and went to bed at 10:00 p.m. I got up again at 2:00 a.m. and drove by a roundabout way to the river mouth, confident that the poachers would have had a telephone call telling them that I was safely asleep many miles away.

I was following a narrow bush road, and, when I got near the rendezvous, I switched out my lights. About a quarter of a mile short of my destination, I stopped the car and went ahead on foot. I scrambled down the bank and looked instantly across the oily water and, as I expected, there was a net, the floats bobbing in the current and reflecting the faint light of the stars.

I decided that the poachers would be camped out not too far away waiting for the dawn, when they would lift their net and be off to peddle their toothsome catch. Slowly the hours passed, as I squatted at the roots of the willow to which the line was tied, with my feet almost in the water. I had left my side arm where it usually was – in the car.

Finally, a bird cheeped in the bush – it was August and bird song was over for the season. Then a flight of ducks whistled overhead. The first grey of dawn put out the stars one by one and I was getting sleepy. I yawned and splashed the cold water on my face. Daylight came up pink and lovely, touching the fog which now began to enshroud the river. I strained my ears. Again, a yellow warbler cheeped. Then silence. Then "Quack!" and a duck rose noisily upstream. I stiffened. All at once, the low murmur of voices, urgent, then the creak of muffled rowlocks. They were coming.

Three hundred yards upstream was a sandbar island grown over with willows where they had obviously spent the night. The rowboat came closer and I could dimly see two men, then the fog shut down. By the sound they were freeing the net at the other end, straight across from me, and I saw the floats wheel away to my right in a mass of froth as it drifted off – the current at the confluence of the rivers was very strong.

Suddenly, the boat and its occupants loomed out of the pink fog within twelve feet of me, the men hauling themselves hand over hand by the net line. Six feet – I didn't move. Three feet – holding the willow roots with one hand, I grabbed the gunwale with my right, pulling in the boat until the keel squidged into the muddy bank.

"All right, boys," I said, "step out. You are under arrest."

I felt my foot slip in the mud and had to take my eyes off the men for a second. *Wham!* Something hit me on the side of the head and the river took me.

I remember wondering what had hit me – whether it was the rebound of the willow or an oar wielded by one of the men. I think the latter, for I subsequently found I was badly bruised with what might have been a sharp edge, but I could not swear to it, although I had recognized one man as a fellow whom I had found troublesome when I had been taking spawn at Fish Creek camp earlier that year. The other man was a fair-haired youngster I had never seen before.

When I came up, I was in the deep shore channel of the Saskatchewan, treading water. As I cleared my eyes, I could see the boat disappearing rapidly across the wide river, making for the north shore. With the help of the current, I soon made it to a wooded island and, following its shore, I found a place where the channel was fairly narrow and, taking to the water again, was able to land near my car. I was thankful to be alive, for the currents in that river are notoriously dangerous.

I was bitterly cold and at once lit a fire to dry my clothes. Fortunately, in the car there was a blanket, which I wrapped around me. As I was redressing, I heard the mournful whistle of the seven o'clock freight as it slowed for the little town across the river. I drove as fast as I could across the bridge four miles north. The town was still sleeping but a section man told me that two men had stood by the tracks as the train approached; later, one young man had walked the ties going north, so he guessed the other must have "jumped the freight."

I drove down to the river bank and finally found the abandoned rowboat, the nets and fish still in it. The latter I loaded in the back of my car, but the boat I filled with rocks, and pushed into the current to sink.

At Battleford, I finally spotted the young man driving a red and white jalopy across the bridge. After some questioning, he admitted his part. He said he was from Saskatoon and that he had met the older man in a beer parlour and thought it would be fun to "do a little fishing."

He was convicted and let off with a nominal fine. I pointed out to him that it was a serious offence to impede an officer, and also an offence not to go to the aid of what might be a drowning man. He replied – rather too pertly – that he did not see me in the water, but he certainly had had a good scare, which I hope he remembered.

I also laid a charge against the other man and swore out a warrant for his arrest. Information was wired to all the RCMP detachments throughout the province, but somehow he slipped through and nothing more was heard of him for the time being.

Two years almost to the day were to pass before, at a country fair many miles away, I recognized the man. I arrested him and escorted him to North Battleford. Apparently, he had fled to Minnesota and only returned when a lawyer there informed him that under the Statute of Limitations he would be free from prosecution in two years. What he did not know was that, since I had recognized him, I'd been able to lay a charge and swear out a warrant, thus technically commencing court proceedings against him, short-circuiting the Statute of Limitations. The gist of it was that the fellow wound up sentenced to a jail term.

XIII

BLACKMAIL AND BLACK NIGHTS

THE TOUCHY THING ABOUT a lot of my work was that, generally speaking, I was not concerned with what might properly be called "criminals." With a few exceptions, the people I was dealing with were normal, ordinary men or women. The hunter who shot a moose out of season would not have stolen his neighbour's pocket book, and the night-poaching fisherman would not have gone by night to raid his friend's hen house. Of course, there were exceptions, and I had to deal with people who purveyed stolen meat and owned illicit stills, but these were only that fair and unavoidable percentage which would be found in any cross-section of society.

Unhappily, as I have said, I did meet with the occasional person who really was a criminal. On one occasion, I had a blackmail attempt made against me which shows the wisdom of using the utmost prudence at all times.

I had to see a man I didn't know about a routine matter and, as I was starting out on a tour of inspection which would include a visit to the man in question, a friend of mine asked if he could come with me as he wanted to take some photographs of rural scenes.

I was glad to have company and we set out. Within an hour, dark clouds were overhead and it looked like my friend's photo-taking would be washed out.

By the time we found the place I was looking for and drew up in front of the house, it was pouring and my friend said, "I'll just sit here and read."

I knocked at the screen door – the inner door was open – and I could see a woman working in the kitchen. I stepped back to avoid the water which was cascading from the roof. The woman asked what I wanted.

"May I come in?" I asked. "I'm getting awfully wet." She didn't reply, so I pulled open the screen door and entered, hanging my dripping hat on a chair and putting my briefcase on the table.

"Sorry to be so abrupt," I said, "but it really *is* raining."

In most cases in these circumstances, a woman would have smiled and said, "That's perfectly all right," but this woman did not reply.

I told her what I wanted, but she said her husband had gone to town and she didn't know when he'd get back.

I told her to give a message to her husband, she agreed and I left.

Later that year – I think it was early November – I drove into what was the market town for these people. When I went to the Chinese café for supper, I found the place full of big, fur-coated farmers who had been delivering wheat to the elevators. They were now enjoying a cup of coffee and a slice of pie before starting back to their homes. I knew most of them and there were the usual friendly greetings and recognitions.

I squeezed through the press and found a newly abandoned booth in the back. My supper had just been plunked down and I had just seized my knife and fork when man edged into the seat opposite. He was a stranger to me.

I nodded, but he just looked at me. He was a small man of indeterminate age with mouse-coloured hair and washed-out eyes. He was in need of a shave and his teeth were stained with chewing tobacco, as were the corners of his lips.

He spoke. "Reckon you're the game guardian?"

I replied, "I am. My name is Symons. Who are you, and what can I do for you?" I half rose, expecting to shake hands as he in turn introduced himself. He made no move, however, and I sat down.

Finally he said, "Well, that all depends."

"Depends on what?" I asked. "I want to eat my supper, and if there is something you want – well, tell me. If not, why did you ask who I was? I've told you my name. Now tell me yours."

"My name don't make no difference," he said softly, his red-rimmed eyes averted.

"Well," I said, "if that's the case, don't waste my time."

I was hungry and becoming irritated with his insolence. I didn't like his shifty eyes and his air of listening, with his head hunched into his shoulders, his jaw out-thrust and his head on one side in a knowing way. He looked at once cunning, ingratiating and intensely suspicious.

"Come now," I said, "if you have anything to see me about, out with it. If not, and you're not here to eat, you can make yourself scarce."

He squirmed his shoulders and leaned over the table. "Mister," he said, "looks like you know a lot of the boys here. Well, how'd you like it if I told them you warn't to be trusted 'round their gals and wimmin-folk, eh?" He leaned still closer and his breath was sour. "See what I mean? Remember the time you tried t'insult my wife when I was away?"

"I certainly do *not*!"

"Not so loud, mister. You certainly do – remember how it rained and you forced your way into the kitchen? Don't worry, my missus told me all about it and the courts 'ull always believe a woman."

I had only vague memories of such a visit, but knew I had better humour this chap a bit. I said, "What if I do?"

"Well, mister, I reckon it's worth two hundred dollars to you if that there story's forgotten."

"And if I tell you to go to hell?"

"Aw shucks, now, there's lots of fellers here and I got a mouth, ain't I?" he leered.

"Okay," I said, "how about a cheque?" I began to get out my chequebook.

He put up his hand and his voice got lower. "Think I'm a damn fool, mister? Nothing doing – cash!"

"Well," I said, "I'll see if the café can cash a cheque. You stay here."

I left him looking rather pleased – not that it made his ugly features look any more attractive.

Quietly, I pushed through the farmers to the desk by the door. "Charlie," I said softly to the beaming owner, "just pass over the 'phone, will you?"

He did so. There were no dial 'phones then so Central answered, "Number, please?"

I said, "Get me the RCMP – and quick."

Presently, I heard the voice of the young constable in charge of the detachment. "Look, Ted," I said, "put your gun on and come to the Daylight Café pronto. Come straight to the back right-hand booth. Don't ask questions now. Got it?"

"Okay." I heard the receiver click up. I went back to the booth.

"Got the money?" The man spoke furtively, nervously – I sensed his nerve was breaking.

"Charlie can't cash it yet," I said, "but he thinks he'll be able to as soon as the boys pay up. We'll have to wait a bit."

The next minute, it seemed, we heard the tinkle of spurs. My man started to slip out of the seat. The policeman was in front of him and he started to duck under the constable's arm, but I said, "Okay, hold it!" and the law had the fellow in a nice firm grip.

I said, "Let's go over to the detachment." I turned to Charlie. "Throw out that grub, Charlie, it's cold. I'll be back after a while."

Charlie's head wagged in puzzlement and the farmers watched us go but said nothing, moving silently to one side to let us through.

As we reached the street and slammed-to the door, we could hear the silence within broken by a hubbub of hearty, speculative voices. We marched in silence to the barracks and bundled the fellow into a chair.

My memory had been working full bat now, and I guessed who the man was but still could not remember his name.

In that peculiarly soft and disarming voice which members of the force are wont to use, the young constable questioned me.

I told him, all but the name. However, the now thoroughly frightened man soon supplied that and it filled up the gap in my memory perfectly. I could see the rain and hear my friend grumbling and visualize that farm kitchen and the woman's dull face.

I finished up, "and just to set your mind at rest, Constable, a man you know – Mr. X. of Y. – was with me. He sat in the car and could see through the screen door."

The constable had naturally made notes of everything, and he now turned to the culprit, who was in a bad state of nerves, and looked at him hard.

Finally the man whined, "I didn't mean nothing, Sarge – I was having a little joke."

The constable, who didn't like being called "sergeant," although he wouldn't have minded being one, looked at him again harder, as if he was thinking.

By this time, the man was practically in a state of collapse.

The policeman spoke to me. "Want to charge him?"

I shook my head.

The policeman spoke again to the wretched man. "Mr. Symons doesn't want to charge you. You are lucky. Now, get out of here, and I mean *get out*! And don't let's see your ugly mug again or by the Lord Harry you'll be a sorry man."

The fellow slunk off and Ted and I went back to a hot beefsteak apiece – on me.

More typically, as I've said, my "culprits" were basically good people.

I never see a canary in a cage but my mind goes back to a tragic happening involving one such person.

A young man, newly married, insisted on taking a chance at illegal fishing. He had a small farm near a lake and I knew him quite well and liked him, but I was almost certain that he was putting in nets, so one day I took him aside and told him point blank that he should not waste his time like that nor allow himself to be persuaded or dared into taking risks, especially in view of his new responsibilities. He seemed to be equally frank and, while neither admitting nor denying anything, told me his thoughts were along the same lines. For his wife's sake, if for no other reason, he had decided it wasn't worth while to "mess about" at night before the season opened.

Two weeks before that date, I had occasion to pass his buildings at dawn and something, I don't know what, caused me to turn in. A light burned in the kitchen window facing the lake. I knocked at the door and the young wife asked me in. I could see she was agitated, so I asked her if anything was the matter.

She tried to compose herself and then quite suddenly broke down. I couldn't bear to look at her as she sobbed out her fears, and kept my eyes on the pet canary which kept jumping from perch to perch. The girl said she was frantic with worry. Her husband had gone out on the lake just after dusk. He had been in the habit of fishing in a bay three miles away and usually got back well before daylight, but today she'd seen nothing of him – he wasn't back and she knew the ice was thin, and she was afraid. By the time she had finished, I'd counted every feather on that canary.

I told her not to worry too much, that perhaps he had seen or heard me and was hiding up in some coulee. I said I would go to look for him. I added, "But you do put me in a bad position, because I shall probably run into him, and then I would have to charge him."

"Oh," she cried, "as long as he's alive I don't even care if he goes to jail! Goodness knows how we'd ever pay a fine, but, oh, do try and do something!"

I promised to go at once and left the house. I roused up a couple of the neighbours and we went down to the bay. I was hoping all the time that we would meet him, but all we saw was a lone coyote loping easily across the ice.

Daylight was broad by the time we scrambled down the steep hillside to the green ice below. We found a couple of nets and a newly-picked ice hole much larger than it should have been and surrounded by two or three inches of overflow water just freezing to slush.

We got the boy out, but life had left him. His ice pick still lay in seven feet of water looking like some sinister weapon of war as it lay on the moon-white sand.

It was a sad return. The neighbours were kindness itself to the young widow and her baby. They took her to one of their houses, comforting her in a clumsy, patient way. They milked her cows and separated the milk, feeding the pigs with the skim, and carefully put the cream in the big can which, when full, would go to town. (A "cream cheque" was very precious in "them days.") For a week they did her chores and then they chipped in with the rest of the community for a gift of cash to help her over the winter.

There was another good man who had turned to illegal ways, a farmer who used to come into one of the Indian reserves from the rough country to the east. His object was to get illegal fish from the Indians, but I had no proof that he traded liquor, although unlawful stills were known to be in those hills to the east.

He was quite an old chap and used a team and sleigh. I heard that he had made a couple of trips and, since I understood that he usually drove on a stormy night so that his tracks would be covered, I decided to make a patrol the next time a snowstorm blew up, which happened a few days later. Knowing that he would not risk coming in the daytime, I started out just after dark. It was about fifteen miles to the east side of the reserve and it was much later than I intended when I got there because of an unforeseen holdup.

As I crossed a stubble field, I felt Monte's shod hooves grate on what at first I thought must be stones, but this was well cultivated land and I wondered why the farmer should have left stones around, and that led to the thought that they might be something else.

It was a black night and the snow was coming down sixteen to the dozen. However, I dismounted and began to kick about in the foot-deep snow. Presently, I hit something which made my foot tingle. I grubbed around – a frozen whitefish. I got out my pocket torch, and by its light I made out a sleigh trail and understood the trick. Someone, hard-pressed to conceal a load of fish, had driven straight across the field throwing fish right and left so that they lay about three to the square yard. These fish, of course, sank out of sight in the soft snow, and the poacher was probably more than happy to see this new snowfall which would completely obliterate all signs.

I realized that he must have some sort of marker for finding the fish again and I was quite right. Following the track, I came head on to a straw stack. Turning back I followed the track again and it went straight as a die to a gate. I knew he could find those fish again – and so could I. I determined I would keep an eye on this field in days to come, but not tonight – I had others of the finny tribe to fry.

Anyway, this discovery had delayed me and it was nearly midnight when I got to the east boundary of the reserve. I thought that, if this was his night, my man would probably be at one of the cluster of Indian buildings by now, so I decided to ride around the boundary all night and be able to "cut" the track of anyone going out, as it was snowing hard and his in-track might already be covered; some Indian, too, might have gone back to the reserve in the evening, but not very likely *out* on a night like this one, and so any track going out would probably be my man.

The boundary was seven miles long with no graded road and bisected by I don't know how many trails crossing it at intervals and spider-webbing out to all points of the compass. So I started at the south and jogged north in the snowstorm, scanning each cross-trail I came to. Fortunately, it wasn't very cold – it rarely is when the flakes fall from a windless sky, big and fluffy like white moths – but I must confess I kept one ear open for that sudden shrill puff which would herald a Nor'wester starting up; if I heard that, I'd know a blizzard was in the making and I'd have to give Monte his head and leave him to find a hut or farm building in the clever way horses have. But it stayed windless and I reached the north end and then back to the south again and saw no sign of a sleigh trail.

I thought I'd make one more patrol at least, and turned north again. In about three miles I ran into a fresh sleigh track just beginning to fill with snow. I dismounted to investigate. The track was going east. I started to follow it and saw something dark – fresh horse droppings just starting to freeze. The team couldn't be far ahead, and I listened for sleigh runners or the jangle of harness, but the snow muffled all sound and I rode on. For six miles or so, the trail wound between poplar bluffs which showed vaguely on either hand. It was not easy to see the tracks and I made but slow time of it.

I was almost sure there should be some buildings ahead. A Metis family lived hereabouts – pretty decent people – and I doubted if my man would travel all night. He'd probably look for a place to stop.

Presently, Monte turned sharp right, ears pricked up, and I was among some crude buildings. There was no light. This looked like the end of the trail – the man would have to feed and rest his horses somewhere. I rode up to the barn huddled against the bush, pushed the door open, slipped in and used my torch. Horses were stamping and blowing.

The farmer's team was next to the door. They were dry but beyond them the air smoked. There in the farther stall was a team of matched greys munching hay and blowing over it. Wet, hot and steaming, it was easy to see that they had only recently come off the trail. On the heel post behind them hung a set of heavy harness with "Yankee britching" which was still warm and wet. Monte wanted in and nudged me with his frosty muzzle, but I said, "Wait a bit, boy," and left him with the reins down – I knew he would not move.

I wanted to locate the sleigh and finally I found it snuggled into a little open space between the trees well back from the barn. It was full to the top of the three-foot wagon box with frozen whitefish.

Evidently, the teamster must be in the shack and I would have to wake the house, but first I went back to Monte, who greeted me with his usual low whinny. I put him in, gave him an armful of hay and loosened the cinch. As I went to the shack, I noticed that the snow was not coming down quite so hard and I could barely see a shrouded moon high in the sky. It was getting colder too.

My knock, twice repeated, was answered by a sleepy-eyed Metis man in his underwear. He looked very uncomfortable as he let me in and lit the smudgy coal oil lamp. True to western hospitality, he then began to shove wood into the big stove and opened the draughts. Then he faced me.

"Well," I said, "sorry to disturb you, Nap, but I guess you know what I'm here for. Whoever the fellow is, let him sleep on. You might as well go back to bed. I'll sit up here."

"Look," he replied, "I know what you're after all right, but I don't know anything else, me. Fellow wants to come in out of a storm – what 'ud *you* do?"

"Let him in," I said, "same as you, and I wouldn't ask questions either. Don't worry – I won't make any trouble for you."

He seemed relieved. He had been a blacksmith and had often shod my horses, but hard times and lack of customers had persuaded him to try farming.

Just then his wife came out and suggested a cup of tea. She wore a floppy pink wrapper tied around the middle with an old tie, but she looked none the worse for that.

Nap said, "Look, it's nearly six o'clock – let's have breakfast."

I was agreeable enough. I was pretty hungry with that almost aching hunger which comes at the approach of dawn after a night out. So she made breakfast, and about the time we were finishing our second cup of tea my man stumbled out of the bedroom. He didn't like it when I told him the team and sleigh plus the fish were under seizure and he was under arrest.

I turned to pay Nap's wife for horse-bait and breakfast – her husband had already gone out to his morning chores. Then I had to be shown the children, which took my attention for a minute or two, and when I turned around the fish peddler was gone.

I went out. The team was still in the barn, so I went behind the brush to the sleigh, and there was the man on top of the load throwing fish right and left into the deep snow. He had his back to me and didn't see me.

"Hold it!" I called out. "You won't save many fish that way and they're government property now, as I told you. Want to make things worse for yourself? You'll just have to load them again."

He turned and saw me. "My mistake, I guess," he said quite civilly, and jumping down began to hunt through the snow and throw them back.

"What were you going to do with them?" I asked.

"Peddle them, of course," he replied. "You know, my son does most of the farm work now – the farm's way east of here – and I really enjoy visiting around the settlements. It gives me something to do, as well as making some money."

He was an oldish man of that tall, spare, sinewy type that can never be idle. His rugged face was set off by a white moustache. I recognized a real free-enterpriser type – a type that scorns municipal aid – a type I cannot but admire.

It really went against the grain to prosecute this decent old fellow, but I had the good of the lake to consider and I had to escort him and his load to the nearest town. He took it like a good sportsman and after the season opened came to bid on a couple of tons of confiscated fish. I hope he made a tidy profit.

I never knew whether he was the same man who had found it prudent to jettison the fish in the stubble field – he certainly knew about unloading in snow, but although subsequently I haunted that field I never found the culprit. Once, while I watched, a truck drew up by the fence, but I had no cover and when he turned his lights across the field the full glare must have outlined me, for he got out of there in a hurry. Eventually, I hired a team and sleigh and gathered the fish myself.

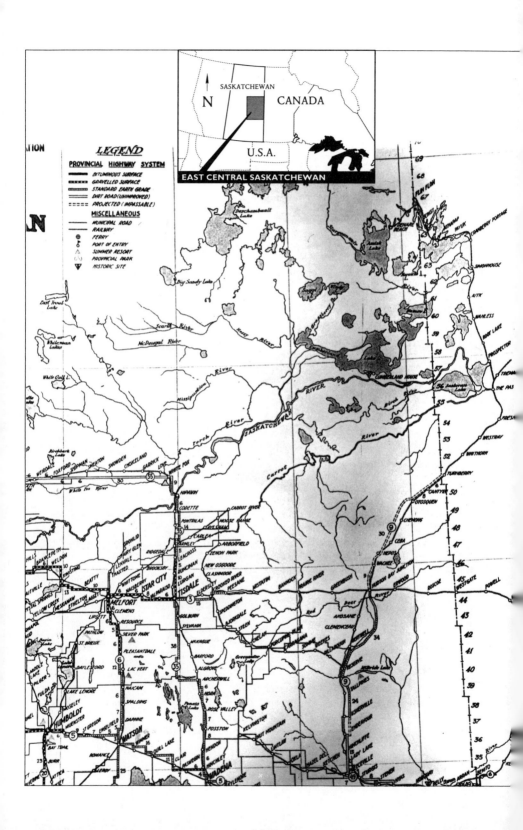

XIV

A NEW POSTING TO THE NORTH

I GOT WORD FROM my superiors that I was to move in the fall of 1936 to Mountain Cabin, a patrol station all the way across the province on the Carrot River, which I was to organize as headquarters for game enforcement in the Pasquia Hills Forest and Game Reserve. I would report directly to the deputy minister at Regina, but copies of my reports would go to the district office at Hudson Bay Junction.

There was at that time no road north from the Junction, nor any road east of Carrot River town or west of the Manitoba border, so the best way to get to Mountain Cabin was by rail to The Pas in Manitoba and thence west up the Carrot River by boat, or by wagon up The Pas Lumber Company's tote road (which was not bad in winter, but a terrible boghole in summer).

There had once been a Dominion Forestry road called the Green-bush Trail which crossed the Pasquia Hills and connected the railway on the south with the Carrot River. This trail came out near the

Sipanok Channel, a waterway which linked the North Saskatchewan River with the Carrot. When flood water came down the Saskatchewan, this channel took the overflow to the Carrot, and it was this annual "flood" in the latter river which was depended upon by The Pas Lumber Company to bring down the winter's cut of logs to their big mill at The Pas.

I was therefore to take train for The Pas and wait there till the department sent saddle and pack horses from Regina. These would take me and my supplies to my headquarters, which was situated on the banks of the Carrot some sixty miles west (which means about forty miles by road west of the Manitoba border). By boat, it was a good deal more due to the winding of the river. I hated to part with Monte and Bill, but they had earned an easier life and both were sold to a friend who would care for them well.

By now, things had quietened down considerably on the game and fish front in the Battleford area, and I felt reasonably pleased at the increase in game and fish of all kinds.

My two last cases at Battleford were actually "test" cases which, if successful, would set a pattern for future tightening up of enforcement.

The law was definite about the illegality of catching fur bearing animals (principally coyotes) in snares, and the ordinances went on to make it an offence for a fur dealer (or anyone else) to have in his possession the pelt of any such animal which had been snared.

However, the enforcement arm had always had to be cautious about laying charges in such cases, for the lawyers could make it very uncomfortable. Very often, the evidence of snaring was hard to see on the outside of a pelt, and it was necessary to turn the skin inside out, revealing the congestion and discolouration of the neck part and the varying degrees of cutting in the skin itself. I usually felt through the neck and throat fur of suspected pelts with my fingers; if I felt a small hole or slit or what might be stitches, I would then investigate further. Anyone who has ever turned a stiff "cased" pelt inside out after it was dry will know that it is not pleasant work. Coyote, wolf and lynx pelts have a strong and offensive odour which, combined with the dust from the furs, makes one sneeze, and the job is that much worse in a grubby, ill-lit warehouse with a fur dealer and his clerks ribbing you, threatening you for damage and making a general fuss. This didn't always happen, of course; many fur dealers were very well behaved and patient, but there were the others.

In one city, I had to go through seven hundred pelts, and out of this bunch I picked about twenty pelts which were typical of snared animals. One or two had the skin of the neck completely cut by the wire and the trapper had sewed it back together. However, I knew a lawyer would say something like: "I submit to the court that there is no evidence at all to show that this animal was snared. The man who trapped it had a perfect right to chop its head off and then sew it back on again if he wished."

At one stage in this investigation, my superiors suggested that the case should be dropped, but I gave them a report which decided them to back me up and I was permitted the assistance of Crown counsel.

The Crown in this case obtained a conviction and it did a world of good, but it had cost me a lot of hard work and many miles of travel. First of all, I went through the dealer's books and found the names of several trappers whom I suspected of snaring. Of course, you could not depend on these books with dishonest dealers, nor could you determine which particular pelt came from which trapper; the books were only supposed to keep a record of the number and kinds of pelts purchased.

In order to make comparisons, I was able to obtain from a judge a *duces tecum* subpoena which allowed me to go through the dealer's private records. I made a fine discovery by this means. I had taken the precaution of asking for a RCMP officer to accompany me as a witness and I found at least two entries that showed not only payments for pelts to trappers but also sales of snare wire, which was not allowed to be sold in Saskatchewan.

I then visited some of the trappers and found one who was prepared to admit that he had sold snared coyotes to the dealer. In further support of my case, I brought in two of the best trappers in the north to give evidence, and also a retired Hudson's Bay Company's post manager whose opinion would be acceptable.

The dealer turned to me after the trial and said rather bitterly, "How do you expect me to know a snared pelt? I buy them in good faith."

I said, "You have been a fur dealer much longer than I have been a game guardian. I know how, and so should you."

The other case was of much the same nature. This time, it was to do with a man who had a government contract to supply fish. I had seen some of his fish and I knew by looking at them that they had been caught before the season opened. I had made it so dangerous to try to transport and sell fish in the closed season that inveterate poachers had been trying a new dodge by leaving the fish under the snow in the woods and waiting until after the season opened to move them.

That had just about become a thing of the past, too, but here I found it starting up again and I would have to do something. Again, my superiors became timid, but I won out with the help of evidence from several experienced fishermen and another valuable ally who was the manager of a fish company in Manitoba. This, combined with my own evidence, did the trick and broke down one more barrier behind which illegal operators had felt safe.

The evidence in this case was the condition of the fish; no one catching fish in the legal season would chuck them to freeze together in a haystack or poplar bluff, yet the grass, dead leaves and twigs adhering to them was certainly *prima facie* evidence of where they had been. Then again, the broken-off fins and tails showed they had been handled roughly after freezing, as they would be if dug out of a snowdrift. Still again, there were shovel marks on many of them, and the dark colour of their heads and bellies bespoke a strong thaw which had occurred just before the season opened. Lastly, their bellies were full of yellow spawn which had, before freezing, oozed out among them.

When I laid half a dozen of these fish alongside some neatly frozen, silver and intact fish which had been legally caught and put in a shed to freeze, the contrast really impressed the court. There was no doubt this man had had some Indians storing up fish for him, as he lived alongside a reserve and had daily contact with them.

The defence was along the usual lines. This man had a licence to fish and had availed himself of it; what he did with his catch or where he stored it was *his* business, and how could anyone prove that all the whitefish in a lake were spawned out by December 15? However, the defence was overruled – and a good thing too.

I felt these cases to be a good wind-up to my activities in this area. It galled me to think that the public had the idea that a man had to be caught in the act before he could be convicted and that game officers were not expected to make a thorough investigation and to gather evidence with as much care as a police officer would regarding stolen goods or narcotics.

The night before I left Battleford, I was visited by a deputation of commercial fishermen who took me to the village hall and, after a few appropriate words of commendation for my work, presented me with a large and handsome Gladstone bag of cowhide.

They surrounded me and shook hands – dark-eyed Frenchmen

and blond Swedes, most of whom I had at some time or other taken to court.

To cover my feelings, I could only say jokingly that it wasn't apparent to me whether the gift was an expression of appreciation of my work or of relief at my departure!

To this day, I still have the bag, which has travelled many miles with me in several countries, and it is a constant reminder to me of those tough and reckless men who had played their game as I had played mine, with no anger nor hatred.

The same day, my replacement, George Revelle, arrived. He confided to me, "I don't want to say why, Bob, but you'll find out the newfangled department is not the old Game Branch, and they don't want to understand *protection* as we know it. I know you'll take orders from the deputy and he's a good chap – but I'm afraid it won't help much. The Forestry is sitting in the saddle up there, and you'll have a rough time."

I thanked him.

I shall write only briefly about my time in our northern wonderland, as much has been written already about this part of our country.

It was late fall when I finally arrived at the set of untidy log buildings which was the Mountain Cabin Ranger Station. The previous ranger was an untidy and slovenly man, and I was shocked at the growth of knee-high weeds all over the small clearing in the heavy bush. I felt even more depressed when I discovered the slops and rusty tin cans of years which lay where they had been thrown away among these weeds.

I had been allowed to hire a man, a highly recommended Indian, who would take care of the horses, dogs and equipment and also occasionally accompany me on patrols where an extra hand might be needed to paddle one of the two canoes or to cut out trails and get wood.

No one lived within twenty miles. My nearest neighbour was on the Manitoba border and there was The Pas Lumber Company's Camp Six, thirty miles up river. Cumberland House lay on the Saskatchewan a two-day trip to the north and the town of Hudson Bay Junction (now known simply as Hudson Bay) about the same distance south, but there was no trail – and, indeed, not even a blaze – from Mountain Cabin over "the hump" at that point. All was an untracked wilderness of wild and rugged scenery – deep canyons, rushing torrents, dark muskegs and shaggy forest.

Freeze-up and snow came within a week of my settling in and some days later I made a trip into The Pas for mail and to post reports. That was when I met Laurie Phinney, an ex-Flying Corps officer, who was superintendent of fish and game for Northern Manitoba. We took to each other, and I was introduced to one of his officers with whom we discussed the possibility of joint patrols on the provincial boundary.

On my return, my hired man, Babe, told me that my train of dogs had arrived and was in the old log barn. These had been purchased by order of the deputy minister from a well-known breeder of Huskies in the Nipawin country. They had been delivered the day before by way of The Pas Lumber Company, which had a snowmobile at their camp.

Next morning, I got the toboggan and harness ready and went to take the dogs for a trial run. I didn't know much about Huskies then and I didn't like the way they roared in chorus when I opened the barn door! In the dusk of the building, six pairs of eyes gleamed like green jewels and the clamour was awful. They were chained to the wall far enough apart to prevent fighting, and as I approached they set back their ears, wrinkled their lips to show business-like teeth and growled in unison from the very bottom of their throats.

"Well, boys," I said, "it's no use me looking at you, and I'll have to name you."

I let them just see the cariboo dog whip tucked into my belt. Babe had told me the one nearest to the door was the wheel dog and the big grey one farthest back was supposed to be the leader, so I walked straight up to the first as nonchalantly as I could, seeing that his whole body shook with a rumbling growl and he was straining at his chain.

"Come on, boy," I said as firmly as possible, wishing it was an outlaw horse. I kept my eyes on him and grabbed his collar. The growling stopped and he made no resistance when I undid the chain from the staple and led him out. I slipped the collar over his head and did up the belly-band. The toboggan was, of course, tied to a tree so that he couldn't get away. Forever after, the wheel dog was called "Boy."

I repeated the process with each dog in turn, naming them as I harnessed them "Sky," "Peesoo" (lynx, since he looked like one), "Sport," "Croppy" (for his ears) and finally "Grey" (the leader).

I untied the toboggan, grasped the trail rope and cracked my whip as I stepped on to the bow-end of the toboggan. Away we went down the trail, wheeled about two miles and returned, every bushy tail up and tongues lolling in a joyous grin. They were pups – brothers – and they had been raised in a dog enclosure and so had seen few people but their attendant. They had a lot to learn and I was not the best teacher, but we got acquainted, and many, many miles did I subsequently make with them over wind-swept muskegs and through deep and log-strewn bush.

The joint patrols worked well. I would meet the Manitoba man at Murphy Cabin on the boundary and he would usually bring my mail from The Pas and we were able to apprehend several of the Manitoba poachers.

On one occasion, we followed up a horse toboggan track from my side and came to a set of buildings. The people were new settlers – Finlanders – and were a numerous family which included several tough-looking young men.

Our search ended in a bedroom over which a young woman stood guard. She said we must not go in, for her grandmother was ill and in bed; but we'd found the head of a fat moose calf by their trail in some woods and the rest of it must be somewhere, for the bloody toboggan stood empty in the yard, so I suggested that I would just look in the door. This I did, over the woman's shoulder.

There was a big lump in the bed and I watched it closely. Not a sign of breathing. I stepped in and touched the quilt over grandma's shoulder. She was evidently beyond human aid, so I told the girl to turn back the covers a bit. Grandma was very dead indeed – she was the fat moose calf we were looking for and the bedclothes were in a horrible mess.

No charge was laid; they were pioneer settlers trying to live. But we told them not to go into Saskatchewan to hunt, for that side was a game reserve, and also *not* to shoot moose cows or calves.

I had to make several trips across the Carrot to Cumberland. The way – there was no trail – led through large patches of tamarack for this terrain is level and largely swampy. Most of the tamaracks were young trees of only about fifteen feet in height. A few bigger ones and some blackened stumps protruding through the snow showed the results of the past fire from which the younger growth sprang.

According to the wonderful rules of nature, each tree was almost exactly equidistant from its neighbour and no orchardist could have ranked them better. Through the soft purplish blur of their whorls of slender branches all set with winter buds, the blue outline of the Pasquia Mountains, as this outthrust of the second steppe was called, crouched like a camel at rest, the hump recognizable as the peak of Wildcat Hill.

Cumberland House was the first inland supply depot for Charles the Second's Company of Adventurers, and was duly proud of itself. At Cumberland was stationed that most intrepid and charming corporal of the famous force – Chappin of the Mounted Police, always called "Chappy." I usually slept at his headquarters and made many a patrol with him.

Two elderly women, sisters, the daughters of a former Hudson's Bay man, had always to be visited, for they were the official issuers of trapping licences and collectors of fur royalties at this point. Very efficient and official was one woman, and very charming was the other. In summer, having tea in their lovely garden, or in winter in the sitting room discussing the same beverage, one would never have believed that one was so many miles from an opera house, a road or a railway.

The sitting room was full of solid evidence of their father's and brother's travels and adventures, from the Bengal tiger skin which draped one wall to the Zulu shields and knobkierries on the other.

Summer was a trying time, although enlivened by the songs of warblers, thrushes and grosbeaks and in spite of the beauty of the ferns and foliage. The almost daily downpours (which brought mosquitoes in such clouds as I never want to see again), followed shortly by hot sunlight, had an enervating effect. (Remember, I was used to dry air and clean, cool prairie winds. But even so, this lassitude in the hot weather I was unable to account for; it led to bouts of some sort of fever, perhaps akin to malaria – I don't know, and neither did the doctor at The Pas.)

I never was particularly allergic to insects – ants didn't bother me, nor wasps buzzing around my head (I knew better than to slap at them), and even the "bulldog" flies and the nasty triangular deer flies did not upset me much. I had hardly noticed the mosquitoes on the prairie, but I have seen them in the swamps of Niska and Shallow Lakes in such number that I admit they drove me to cover.

After the showers, the tree trunks would gleam wetly, turning the dull bark to stronger greens and purples, while the big raindrops would patter-patter down from the forest leaves for anything up to twenty minutes, and the birds – black-throated green warblers and purple finches especially – would sing with renewed fervour after the rein-forced silence.

The dry mellow falls were lovely, and, at that season, I travelled largely by pack and saddle. There would be just that nip of night frost to keep down the insects, and the days would be glorious in royal blue and gold, with the dark spires of evergreens setting off the sky and the forest.

In winter, I took to the dogs again and travelled through a fairyland of interlaced alders topped by immense snow-laden spruce, the silence of the woods only broken by the chattering of an occasional squirrel if it should be mild or the frost noises in the trees if it was cold.

Snow was usually deep, but, except on the open muskegs, wind was not a problem nor drifts a hazard.

By night, I tied the dogs and fed them and then baked my bannock and made my tea. Then, well fed and warm, I would roll up in my sleeping robe with only the stars – that infinite array of distant bright worlds – for my roof.

R.D.S

XV

ROUTES AND RADIOS

IT DIDN'T TAKE ME long to begin to understand what George had hinted to me that last afternoon at Battleford.

Times were definitely changing. A new guard was taking over the administration of fish, game and forestry regulations in Regina and the iron grip of bureaucracy was tightening around the throats of field men like me who were more concerned with animals and patrols than desk and reports. Moreover, a new fascination with technology – even back then! – was beginning to be felt. In an area where forest cover was dense, there was more and more talk of airplane game-counting flights and mathematical calculations; more and more talk of two-way radios, even though weather conditions often made such communication all but impossible.

The new way of thinking had little use for patrols. Horses and dogs – which I was just learning to value – were soon to be replaced with trucks and snowmobiles, and several other schemes were proposed to bring the service more "up to date" and substitute mechanical gadgets for men.

The end of an era was fast approaching.

I can offer no better example of this clash of ideas – old and new – than an extended patrol I made during my first winter at Mountain Cabin.

I had instructions from Regina to look into the feasibility of a route across the hills to Hudson Bay Junction, and I therefore planned to blaze a trail as a preliminary survey for such a route. If this route could be established, it would make it easier – or possible – to send men and equipment from there into the hills.

Shortly after the New Year, therefore, I started out on this enterprise. Babe would stay at Mountain Cabin and care for the horses. It was bitterly cold. Throughout the trip, the temperature was never higher than twenty-five below zero and at night it dropped to thirty-five or forty.

Each morning, I left my dogs in camp and plodded for seven or eight miles on snowshoes, avoiding the steeper hills, finding good crossings on the rivers and keeping out of boggy swamps and big patches of brule – even dogs could not travel through such crisscrossed tangles of fallen trees and later it would be costly work to cut a trail through them. I kept pretty well to the east slope of the hills, which would allow a better grade, although it meant a few more miles as I would have to swing a little easterly and southwesterly to Otosquen, a flag station on the Hudson Bay Railway.

Constantly, I ran into such hazards that I was forced to find another way. The trees here were large and in thick stands, so that anything like a view ahead was out of the question.

Each noon, I turned back, following my tracks, blazing trees, cutting out brush and noting compass bearings using my wartime prismatic instrument. I was also equipped to take rough barometer readings of heights. On this survey, I found that a good deal of the mapping of creeks was incorrect. The upper reaches of the Waskwi had been mistaken for the Thickbush and its confluence with the Niska was entirely misplaced. I was able to correct these and other errors.

So I pursued my happy way with only the grey jays for company, or perhaps a moose which stayed to browse the alders till I was upon it. I saw wolf tracks in profusion, but lupus is shy and I saw none, although sometimes I could hear my dogs back at camp raise their husky howls and knew they had scented their wild cousins.

Once back among my welcoming dogs, I cooked my brief dinner and then hitched them up and said, "Mush!" They strained to the harness and dashed forward, delighting in the twice-tramped trail. It was usually dark, or at least dusk, when we arrived at the end of my morning's work, and I would again make camp and feed my animals their daily ration of dogmeat or fish.

So it went on for almost two weeks, for I ran into so much bad going that my average rate of work trail making was a bare five miles a day. The cold never let up and I was getting very short of dogfood when one afternoon I heard the close whistle of a freight train and felt the ground rumble while the snow fell in clots from the tall spruce. That night, I slept in an abandoned cabin at Otosquen and had the company of one of the section men.

Next day, I mushed the dogs along the railway track, the toboggan bumping from tie to tie, and late that evening saw the lights of Hudson Bay Junction twinkling brighter than any stars. I went to the little lumber hotel and, after a good feed and a hot bath, treated a frostbitten toe and fell asleep in a soft bed.

I reported at the district forestry office next morning. The superintendent was not glad to see me, but I was not too surprised. The superintendent could not reprimand me, for he knew my instructions, but he did say that such a patrol was a senseless waste of time. I remember feeling that I was put in a position similar to that of a coureur de bois up "on the mat" before Intendant Buchesneau in the days of New France – in short, that I was a trespasser in the forest. This was in part due to the fact that the superintendent always used the administrative "we" when talking to his staff.

"We do not consider it advisable," he said after I had submitted my report, "to make new trails. Leave well alone is our policy. If we make trails or build cabins, then the poachers will come in."

"I might agree with that, sir," I replied, "if the poachers had always been kept out – which they have not. You will recall that I routed out a nest of trappers that had occupied that abandoned cabin on the Greenbush Trail for several winters. By patrolling the route I have followed at regular intervals there would be a good chance of cutting across any toboggan track coming from Manitoba – a far better chance than by slowly whacking along through the bush with no real plan."

He went on with his argument. Timber was the thing that really mattered. If we wanted game, why didn't we fence in a township, put in some moose and deer – a few elk if you like – and say, "There's your game!"?

"Anyway," he ended, "if you dash about pinching fellows for hunting and trapping, where will our timber resources be? Those guys will feel mad and they'll simply up and burn the forest, and then we can *all* fold up."

"Well," I countered, "if they'd burn that east side where all the pine is 'red' and the birch overmature, it would do a world of good and there'd be some browse for moose and a stand of decent timber later."

This, I knew, was rank heresy – if not treason – but I never have been able to persuade any of the forestry branch that their "Keep-the-forest-green-or-you'll-have-no-game" slogan, while perhaps good for timber in the short run, is *not* in the interests of game – for where would the animals obtain browse in heavy stands of timber? All good game results from fire. Ask an Indian or an experienced hunter where does he get his best moose – in a heavy spruce stand or in a "burn"?

I took another tack.

Were we – the enforcement arm – to be under the threat of hooligan reprisals? That way the road lay open to intimidation and eventually gangsterism; and, if we did not even have men who could and would apprehend such people, we might as well fold up anyway. I pointed out that if *we* did not fully "occupy" the forest, then these Robin Hoods would – there were plenty of examples in history.

We didn't get anywhere with our conversation – two men at cross-purposes seldom do; but I began to understand why the game reserve was practically trapped out. It never had been fully possessed or controlled and from the look of things was not going to be, in spite of the deputy minister's high hopes – and mine.

Today there is a gravelled road which follows the trail I blazed thirty years ago, although my name has never been connected with it, so soon are things forgotten. But this road was not built to fulfill the purpose behind those two weeks in the bush – the purpose of preserving our wildlife resources. Rather it was put in for the opposite reason – to throw those resources open to the tourists and hunters, for the Pasquia Game Reserve as such no longer exists.

Shortly after I returned to Mountain Cabin, I set about tidying up the old cabin, which had become my office, as well as painting and whitewashing the building. By spring, I had built a new, roomy dwelling house of peeled logs, where I could live in comfort and have my books around. Floor and roof lumber I rafted down river from one of the abandoned lumber camps which the company very kindly put at my disposal.

Later, I dug up with a mattock the stump-strewn area behind the buildings and put in a fine garden, well fenced with whitewashed pickets. Above the office flew the Red Ensign and in front was a strip of lawn, while at the top of the steps from the floating canoe dock was a freshly-painted ten-foot sign which read: "Mountain Cabin Ranger Station."

I had few visitors. Occasionally, the trader from Red Earth dropped in on his way by water to The Pas, once a year Corporal "Chappy" called in, and in the spring the "rearing crew" for the log drive on the river passed by, so I was glad one day to greet Hector MacLeod, the head teamster for the La Pas Lumber Company, and invited him to supper. The grizzled Bruce County Highlander complained bitterly that I no longer let his teams tramp across where my lawn now was, although he gave me grudging recognition for the new trail which detoured around behind the government building and the wagon-park I had laid out. He cheered up after supper and went so far as to say the greensward was "a sight bonnier than them old wagon ruts."

Hector was of the old school – a hard worker, a hard drinker and a wizard with two, four or six horses. He waxed sad over the changes which were pressing hard on those of his craft.

"Aye," he said, "they bulldozers and tractors will be stinking up the woods, I fear. And where will I be – and my horses? Hoot-toot! Will be pulling they fancy contraptions from the muck, I doot. Foreby, d'ye see, just think o' the awfu' damage to the bush! It's horses for the bush if ye dinna want to throw a lot of callants oot o' work and break doon the best o' the young growth as well! It's fair disgusting!" Hector hit the gate post with a stream of tobacco juice.

Sure enough, the company started to dispose of the horses, and among the first to go were the big, clean-limbed drivers which had made nobody knows how many trips to The Pas hospital with injured men, for accidents are common in the woods.

The company had a doctor and an emergency ward at the camp, and here injured men got first aid or perhaps broken limbs set before being sent down river.

The first trip the new hospital bus made took over a week one way. A hundred miles of bush road with no stopping place or repair shop wasn't the best place for experiments. On this occasion, I had to go with the dogs to bring the sick men to my station from two miles west where a breakdown occurred. Meanwhile, at forty below, the driver had to keep a fire going and spend days with tools and then a welding outfit before the vehicle was ready for work again. I could see that when you get modern equipment you must have the whole setup; no use to have rapid transportation unless you have good roads; no use to have rapid communication without good transportation.

When the next freight came up from The Pas, there came with it a big box for me. I opened it. It contained a two-way radio with full instructions and a covering letter to say that I was to be "on the air" every morning at 9:30 a.m. I was to contact the ranger at Carrot River Town and then tune in to Hudson Bay Junction.

Next time I saw the district superintendent, I locked horns with him again. How, I asked, could I make my patrols if I had to be at the office each morning? He replied that he wanted to know what was going on.

"Why, particularly?" I asked.

"Well," he replied, "if you have a fire I want to know at once."

"What good will that do?" I countered. "Say I spot a fire at noon. I have to stick around till nine o'clock next day to tell you, and what help can you give me from the Junction? I have to get my crews and supplies from this end. There was a fire at Fir River last summer – remember? You, with your policy of no roads, didn't even get a crew in. Your men got lost in the bush and then ran out of grub. What finally put the fire out? Freeze-up and snow – that's what!

"Now you propose to take away my patrolman and give me an outboard motor and a lot of other junk. So if I find a fire I have to report it? We used to leave one man at the fire to do what he could and plan an attack, while the other could get a bunch of Indians and some grub at either Red Earth or The Pas and then get right back and go to work. By the time we reported it the fire was out, usually."

"Oh, that's old-fashioned stuff," he said. "Too expensive – men eat a lot of grub and just keep the fire going as long as they get wages. We'd rather put in a bulldozer."

"Okay," I said. "You're the boss. But you can bet the trucks and bulldozers are going to cost plenty too. I've never yet seen any government service who claimed they could operate cheaper that didn't ask for increased estimates, and I never shall. Anyway, if you must use bulldozers why try to lock the stable door after the nags are gone? Why not make grid roads which can help us isolate a fire – roads up which supplies and help can come?"

He changed his tactics. "Well, why can't you see it from the view of personal safety, then? Look, you go out on those long trips and some day you'll turn up missing. Why take chances? Suppose you are around the station and say you break a leg – you could let us know and we would send someone out from The Pas."

That didn't make any sense to me and I told him so. First of all, reception was often very bad and perhaps they couldn't contact The Pas. Surely I could get there as fast as anyone from there could get to me? Unless I was in very bad shape I could get in my canoe or my dog toboggan and be on my way. If I couldn't do that, the chances were I couldn't make it to the radio, and then, if static was too bad . . . .

Anyway, an accident might happen at ten o'clock and I couldn't contact anybody till the next morning – by that time I could be in town.

There was no place for a plane to land – had there been, there might have been meat in his argument.

It would have been better to have had one more patrolman – a machine is a poor substitute for a human being.

I liked the superintendent. He asked me to supper that night and was a genial host, but in line of work we were far from compatible.

Soon after I left Mountain Cabin, I was to learn that my neat set-up had reverted to its old self. The new man did not want a large and comfortable home, but he did want cover for his new love – a big red truck; so he quartered himself in the old office and tore out the front of the fine log house, fitted it with double doors and made the building into a garage.

So one man builds and another destroys.

R.D.Symons.

XVI

Nostalgia and a New Horizon

The many hours of travelling in the rain and the continual sleeping in blankets which, if not wet, were rarely bone-dry, was having its effect on me and bringing on a rheumatic condition which, while no more than a nuisance, is still with me.

After one particularly hard canoe trip, I fell into a fever accompanied by chills and shivering. I went to the hospital at The Pas. The doctors worked hard and patched me up, but it had been what was at one time called "rheumatic fever" and it left me weakened.

While I was at The Pas, a tragic happening was much talked of in the hospital. A lumber company's horse died and was hauled out on the banks of the Saskatchewan, where some young boys found it and conceived the idea of taking off the shoes to sell to the local blacksmith. Unable to remove the nails, two of them went back for a saw to cut off the hooves, leaving one boy at the carcass. A group of sleigh dogs also had designs on the horse and, when the boy attempted to drive them

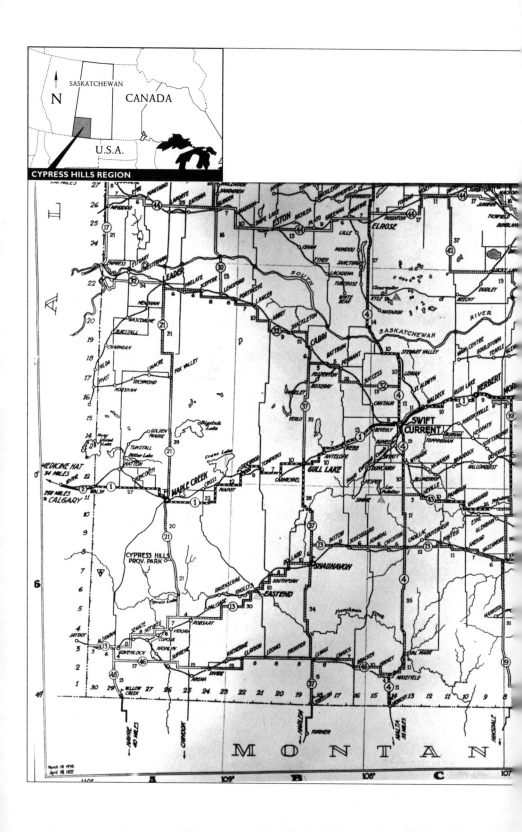

off, they attacked and killed him. Before help arrived, there was little of the lad left but his shoes and belt. As a result of this, the Town Fathers took action and passed an ordinance that all sleigh dogs must be chained in a dog pound under an attendant which they provided. There had been for a long time a law that such dogs could not run at large, but the law had not been enforced strictly enough – how often this is so.

This incident seemed to crystallize for me the changes – not just in the service but in society as a whole that I was witnessing, and, combined with a sense of failure and frustration at Mountain Cabin, my illness depressed me considerably.

I had had great plans for making the Pasquia Forest into the wonderful reservoir for game and fur for which it was so well suited. Here was a splendid untouched area, already supplied with the necessary "seed" – seed of moose and bear; of caribou, deer and elk; of muskrat and beaver, and of the "fine furs" (lynx, fox, marten and fisher). From this protected area, the overflow could restock the northeast fur country and ensure a decent living for the Indians.

However, I was seeing my plans fall to pieces and, although I had done a good deal to stop poaching, I was single-handed and desperately needed a couple of good bushmen. I had made some patrol routes and put up some cabins, but I had hardly touched the fringe of the work which needed to be done.

I planned to renew my efforts, but the doctors had other ideas and they recommended to the deputy minister that I be moved – at least temporarily – to some dryer area in the south of the province. It was therefore arranged that I should go to the West Block of the Cypress Hills, a ranching area with which I had once been familiar.

I said goodbye to my lovely forest with regret. Looking back, I think that my work may not have been quite in vain – no honest work is, I'm sure. But now I realize that so-called "progress" was bound to undo any achievement of mine.

The Pas, too, I was sorry to leave. The most friendly of towns of the north, peaceful and slow, it went its quiet way for a few more years. Like Battleford it was a gentle backwater and I made many friends.

I no sooner got to the south than Hitler's war broke out. I had severed my connection with the militia due to being so isolated, but I offered my services, only to be rejected on account of my age.

The ranger station at Battle Creek was a charming place about four miles upstream from old Fort Walsh. I had always loved the high benchlands and the steep pine-clad slopes filling the air with good scents, while the strong winds from the high plains are spicy with the smell of sage. My health improved rapidly and the joys of riding horseback did much to elevate my spirits.

But here, too, the winds of change, brewed in the bureau at Regina, were beginning to blow. There were plans for a park at the Centre Block and for the building of tourist roads and tourist attractions.

I found, much to my disappointment, that I had no funds for patrols outside the boundaries of the West Block itself, although I was aware of the need for the protective arm among the antelope scattered on the great rolling plains which swept southward to Montana and Wyoming.

Elk had been reintroduced in the hills a few years before, which was a mistake; they are a source of trouble in a settled community and the forays of these big animals were a constant annoyance to the ranchers. It was always a wonder to me that the powers-that-be, if they wanted a large game animal, had not thought of moose. There was plenty of timber and "jungle" here where these animals could thrive, and they would have been content to remain there in their solitary way. Elk, on the other hand, like the open country, as they graze as well as browse. Also, they like to go in herds and move about far more than moose, and were therefore wont to roam far beyond the reserve boundary, wrecking haystacks and trampling crops or, worse, tearing stooks to pieces and scattering sheaves to be rotted by the fall rains.

The elk got so bold that some of the ranchers were at their wits' end. One of them, the late "Bub" Gaff, showed me a great, high stack of oat bundles upon which a band of about a dozen elk fed nightly, and added insult to injury by sleeping on top of this stack so that for many feet down the sheaves were wet and soggy and mucked with dung. "Bub" built his fence stronger and higher to no avail – those big elk either forced it down or scrambled over it. He sat up at night and fired blank cartridges, he hung lighted lanterns on the posts and he chained dogs to the fence – all was to no purpose and the elk waxed fat and sassy. Finally, he made so many complaints that I arranged a deal between him and the department which allowed him free grazing on a section of land in compensation for the damage done by what he called "them government haybalers."

The Saskatchewan Fish and Game League had a branch association at Maple Creek, the shopping town for the Cypress Hills. The year I settled in, the league's annual convention was held in that town, which was to be followed by a dinner at the roomy and comfortable home of a local rancher. The department had given permission for a certain especially aggravating elk bull to be killed and served on this occasion.

The great day arrived and the guests all drove out to the ranch. During the dinner, a doctor from Saskatoon remarked that the elk meat was delicious – "so sweet and savoury." Up spoke the grizzled citizen to whom the animal had been such a nuisance. "Shore ought to be. The critter started on my wife's lavendar bushes and finished up with the sweet peas!"

My relations with the ranchers were of the best and altogether this was a happy period of my career except for one thing. Beyond the regular patrols of an area not exceeding a township and a half, and issuing permits for dry wood, building logs and grazing of stock, I was not kept sufficiently busy. It was almost like retirement and the days went along pleasantly enough, but it didn't really suit me. I had no wish to amble along in green pastures – I felt there were much more creative things to do and new frontiers to be seen.

I used to ride down often to the old Fort Walsh, which over the years had become the headquarters of a ranch. Commissioner Woods of the RCMP was a dreamer who wanted the police to raise their own mounts for the sake of uniformity, and he had succeeded in persuading Ottawa to buy the locations. Even then, a gang of Metis axemen under the foremanship of Barney Montour was engaged in duplicating the old buildings of the 1870s in exact replica, using pine logs from the hills.

It was a fortunate thing that one man had the vision and the push to rebuild and preserve the old fort, which is part of our history.

I think it was the following year when some mares were purchased and the famous horse Onslaught was brought from England. From this nucleus sprang the matched blacks which we are privileged to see when the force puts on its famous Musical Ride, or when Mounties escort such notables as the lieutenant-governor or the Brier Cup winners to the Legislative Building.

This itself was a sign of the times. The horses were to be used hereafter only for purposes of pageantry and pleasure, and already herds of lovely feral animals were being rounded up and trailed or shipped to the packing plants – so if the police had not raised their own mounts they might have had to do without.

The clouds of technology were fast approaching and government was losing touch with the people. Bureaucracy was making decisions and man's partnership with nature would soon be an overlordship which would see every bird and beast and rock and tree in terms only of its value on the counter of suburban interests. They would be *things* – things to be manipulated, counted, experimented with and managed. I was a countryman, with a countryman's values, and the invasion of the countryside, forest and groves by "tourism" and all that goes with it was to me a sign that country life was fast on the decline.

I decided to try once more to find a place where a person could lead a natural life before I became a mere park servant, so I went to Regina and consulted the deputy minister, who saw things as I did in many ways. After several days in that city, I saw even more plainly how the wind blew. Western Canada's rural way of life based on a grain and livestock economy was to disappear. The smaller farm was giving way to far-flung acres which would be worked by men whose families would live in the city. The merchants who supplied the rural dwellers were folding up in the face of the alien supermarkets geared to the bright packages of "junk food."

I was therefore delighted to hear from the deputy minister that he had talked to game officials in British Columbia and that, since they were short-handed, they might consider offering me a position.

In the meantime, I had serious thoughts of trying for the north again and, at the suggestion and on the recommendation of Dewey Soper, a biologist with the department of the interior, made application to Ottawa for the position of park ranger at Wood Buffalo Park, which straddles Northern Alberta and the North West Territories. In reply, I was told there were no vacancies but that, in view of Mr. Soper's recommendation, they would keep my name on file.

I went on with my work. The department was then trapping wild beaver – of which the Cypress Hills were well supplied – and transferring them to northern areas where the animals were scarce. All game had increased considerably throughout the province by this time, and very shortly beaver would be in good supply throughout. It was heartening to see the changes since the early 1920s; the three animals we most feared for – antelope, elk and beaver – were now safe.

I did not have to wait long before I heard from Victoria that they needed an experienced man to take over the detachment at the town of Fort Saint John in the Peace River block, and they offered me this position. I therefore sent in my resignation, but promised to stay where I was until my successor arrived, which took several months.

The year before, I had seen a chance to purchase a small ranch on Battle Creek with the idea of leaving the service and settling down; indeed, I had done considerable work on the place, but at this opportunity I offered it for sale and very soon had a customer. Then I said goodbye to Saskatchewan and took train for the west (glad of the extra bonus which the department had granted me in recognition of my services).

As it turned out, my career as a game warden in British Columbia was to be shortlived and I would soon return to my first love, ranching.

In Fort Saint John, I had the misfortune to work under a man who, while excellent in many things, found it difficult to delegate authority, and wanted to be acquainted in the finest detail with every move made by his men. In other words, he was "snoopy." He expected to be notified before any charge was made, and often ordered cases held over until he could be there in person, and, by his impetuosity and interference, often brought about the loss of a conviction. I, who had lost only one case (and that my first) out of many hundreds in Saskatchewan, had to see no less than two cases "go wrong" and an extremely important one settled by most unsatisfactory arbitration because my inspector took them out of my hands.

I found I had less and less time for patrol. In fact, I could not get out often enough or long enough to know what was really going on. I did know that in a huge area such as I had (from the Peace River to the Sikanni), people would feel fairly safe from observation. I know of no deterrent to poaching that equals a warden continuously turning up in all sorts of unlooked-for spots, and a further advantage is that this is the only way the game warden can follow game signs and know of their movements and abundance.

But the office held me manacled, and I wondered why I was not called an office boy rather than a game warden. The inspector wanted weekly reports on any number of things. I am not a good typist and we had used longhand in Saskatchewan, and my best was not good enough. One typographical error and the inspector sent the whole report back to be retyped.

I was beginning to have an uneasy suspicion that perfect results on paper was what was wanted, rather than results in the field. Typists are easy to get, and good game wardens are not, and to me the idea that one of the qualifications for such a position should be the ability to type is preposterous rather than funny.

The job which I had approached with dedication to certain fundamental principles (of which protection is the most important) was now threatening to turn me into a complaisant civil servant, afraid to act, unable and unwilling to make a decision, content to "draw salary and not stir things up," as certain of my cynical opposite numbers expressed it to me.

All around I could see the same signs. Language was being dehumanized by the new shibboleth-ridden terms which were coming into being. A man building his cottage is now said to be "developing his property"; we cease to hold conversations – we "communicate"; an ordinary car becomes a "transport unit."

In the case of nature, we are no longer to enjoy it in all its beauty – we are to "identify with our environment." We are not to shoot game, we are to "harvest" it (which "resourceswise" is now part of its "multi-use").

History and tradition play less and less part in this "progressive" ideology. I remember a case in which a provincial policeman and I were on a patrol in search of a man accused of stabbing his wife to death.

My companion patted his carbine and said, "Well, this man is an animal, so it's shoot on sight!"

I said, "We can't do that!"

"Why not?" he asked. "He's a murderer, isn't he? He was seen killing his wife."

"No, he's not," I replied, "not until a court says so."

"Oh!" He laughed. "*That stuff!*"

This is not, of course, typical. It was, however, a straw blowing in the wind.

I feared that worse was yet to come. I realized that, so far as wildlife was concerned, what one war and an influx of settlers had done twenty-five years ago was being repeated on a much more threatening scale by the influx of the Brave New World which would reduce everything to the common denominator of the dollar bill.

More and more I longed to be a free man. My mind constantly went back to a peaceful and isolated valley in the west, just below those great mountains which lay blue and bold towards the sunset.

Riding back from a foothills patrol early in my BC stay, I first traversed the valley of Upper Cache Creek. It was a beautiful valley, reminiscent of Battle Creek in the Cypress Hills. There were five miles of well-grassed hillside. There was a flat some five hundred miles across, not too heavily wooded. There were clumps of spruce for building logs and poplar for firewood. There were springs of pure water as well as the looping creek.

I looked at the grasses. There was western and northern wheatgrass to the stirrups, as well as oat-grass and June grass and fescue. I knew the poplar woods would be lush with peavine. I camped at a spring and cooked my lunch, while my saddle horse Duke and my pack mare Toni grazed to fulfillment.

What a place for a cattle ranch! No one within miles. No wagon road, only a rugged and tortuous pack trail.

A small seed had been sown.

Now, I longed to be free to work as I chose, to think as I chose, to speak and live as I chose.

The war was drawing to an end. The miles of vacant land heretofore closed to settlement would soon be open for purchase. I thought still more about the Upper Cache Creek valley.

I could see Fort Saint John becoming a big town – perhaps a city. I saw that honest poplar fuel would be replaced by gas. There was now a bridge on the river, talk of a hardtop road, of a railway station. This was going to mean more "progress" – more cars, more foul smell, more "civilization" with its clangour of commerce and radios blaring futilities.

Already, the Hudson Bay Store had become a "serve yourself," with everything in small quantities and bright packages. The rancher or trapper who came in with a half-yearly order to the tune of hundreds of dollars had to stand aside and await the convenience of the day-to-day shopper.

I wanted no part of it. Life is too short to waste time on anything but the essentials: food, blankets, a house (any kind of a house), my books, my music and the real things of nature were enough.

The mountains, the everlasting hills where the air was pure – these symbolized the real world. Unchanging, they lay, touched by the summer sun to pink and gold, or, in the warm chinook of winter, part-shrouded by the mirage which lifted their battlements above the dull earth and wafted them into fairy cities fit for man's spirit to occupy …. The stag at dawn … the bull moose at dusk, threshing the spotted alders with his velvet antlers … in the stormy night, the hoarse challenging voices of the wolves (tame and gentle beasts compared with the ravenous wolves of money-lenders and bazaar folk)….

I was nearly fifty, but my health was still good. Why should I stay on in an environment which would soon discard me anyway? Better a few years of life – real life – while there was yet time for accomplishment. Security was not happiness nor fulfillment.

I sent in my resignation.

A load was lifted from me, and I felt such a surge of new life and purpose that I saddled up, rode down to the river, and sang like a boy.

Fate had one last trick to play on me.

I made an application for land at Upper Cache Creek and, whilst awaiting a reply, decided to pay a visit on my mother in England – my mother, who I hadn't seen for twenty-seven years.

The war was still on of course, so I needed an exit permit, which I applied for and got, then headed east.

My boat left with the last large convoy. Just before we sailed, the purser handed me a letter. It was from the department of the interior, and offered me the position of superintendent at Wood Buffalo Park in the North West Territories, with quarters and allowances at Fort Smith and a salary that made me gasp.

A year before, I would have jumped at the job of a buffalo ranger, let alone a superintendentship. As it was, I said, "Too late," and wrote declining the position. I gave thanks for Dewey Soper, and realised that "keeping a name on file" did perhaps mean something after all. I had a moment of regret as I sealed the letter – regret for that shining northland and its big hump-backed cattle. But I thought, "I shall have my own park and my own cattle," and I put regrets from my mind.

POSTSCRIPT

I DID NOT KNOW it then, but before me was a new life after my own heart. A life which would renew in me all the faith which I had of late been in danger of losing. I would be able to see that I had stayed too long in one job which, after all, perhaps was not my right metier.

The story of Hope Springs Ranch at Upper Cache Creek is over today, for, after a lapse of years which brought not only financial success but the discovery of talents hardly used, my health decreed a less active life, and brought my retirement to Saskatchewan, my first love.

All creative art, I now realise, must be nurtured in freedom and isolation, and hard physical work is the best medicine to activate the mind.

Today, some twenty years after the period of which I write, I see my earlier fears realized. The clammy hand of bureaucracy is everywhere under the guise of progress and affluence.

The concept of *protection* of wildlife for its own sake, for its right to live, has been lost. The technologists have discovered that wildlife can be exploited into a billion-dollar business – a vast commercial empire.

The one and only valid argument for the conservation of wildlife is on the grounds of the humanities, based on the moral right to live which these creatures have, and our moral duty to preserve as much as possible of their environment in order that they may do so. There is no other possible or moral basis for conservation.

But the technologist has also been discovered by government – always greedy to impress the people with new things, always greedy under such a guise to obtain more control, more revenue.

So the technologist, not the conservationist, has been put in charge of wildlife, and he must be sure that his findings can be used as an encouragement to the tourist trade; so wildlife has lost its rights and is to be enclosed as in a zoo, to be shot at, gazed at, photographed, and to be the object of "research" by thousands of young people who will be subsidized by grants and awards. To be the subject of a thesis or an essay, these creatures must have their private lives invaded, their eggs must chill and their young must go unfed as they are weighed, measured and banded and kept under observation.

Today, the men in charge of wildlife make few patrols – they are kept far too busy with their multitudinous duties attendant on the administration of tourist camps and parks once set aside for birds and animals, but now geared to attract the money spenders.

They are caretakers, publicity agents, propaganda disseminators, but they are *not* game guardians as their title might suggest. It is not their fault and this is no criticism of any of them. Technology does not encourage dedicated men. It wants people it can train to further its ends. There is no room for initiative or personal thinking, nor does the idea of enforcement meet with approval from the sociologists and educators, for here is another field for their interfering fingers. An "information service" is considered the latest thing in the way of "educating" people to a "greater awareness" of their natural environment, and dozens of pamphlets and brochures are written and disseminated to the public by tongue-in-cheek "experts," all written in the same cold and uninspiring terms.

So the Powers That Be, anxious to hasten the urban concept of trade and commerce and the quick establishment of industry, entrust our precious wildlife to men who have never put their heads against a cow's flank or curried a horse, who have never "felt" contact with living, breathing creatures who like us are not only flesh but spirit; to men who are – perhaps unwittingly – agents for that host of firms and individuals who live by the live blood of our wild brothers and sister. Game today is not protected but managed; "harvested" is the key word, for it sounds less bloody than "shooting" or "killing."

Technology and the humanities are not good bedfellows. You cannot worship God and Mammon, and in the long run our war against nature is a sin. The whole concept of civilization is based on cultural and aesthetic values, so originally our method of dealing with wildlife was based on *conservation*.

But you cannot *manage* things of the spirit – things of flesh and blood which are alive – except by capture and enslavement, to the dooming of the things managed.

Ducks want to nest in peace in a place of their own choosing; cow moose, like all mothers, wish to drop their calves in secrecy and not under the "direction" of a bureau or the eye of a biologist. Wildlife is perfectly capable of *managing* itself within those laws which are part of created biology and ecology, and will survive the cyclical ebb and flow.

But wildlife cannot *protect* itself much longer against the power of the commercial world – a world which must sell cars and gasoline, boats and engines, hot dogs and motel space, sports jackets and binoculars, firearms and thermos bottles, fishing tackle and hip waders, ammunition and duck calls, cameras and light filters, hunting knives and cold storage, taxidermy services and college degrees, with the inevitable result that publicly paid conservation men no longer tramp the bush or meet the public face to face in wood and wilderness, but lend themselves to the "sportsmen's programmes" and appear on TV to discuss wildlife in terms of new equipment, new fishing areas and bigger fish, blandly suggesting that to have more game we must kill more game and lure the bull moose within range of the latest telescopic sights by appealing to his love by a faked cow-call from the alder swamp. (The old moose season, which did not start until after the rut, was a season of snow and cold, and tourists from the south did not find it convenient to come to our northland then.)

So the bulldozers must push their way further and further to make straight the way for the swift cars of the destroyers of our environment. The roadside cover is flung back in bleeding ridges, lest a snowdrift hamper a quick return to Minnesota with the mangled carcass prominently displayed, and to feed the vanity – not the stomach – of the man who is playing the game of pioneering which his grandfather lived.

Was it for this that the Master of Life created the moose and the deer and the shining fish?

We who have been betrayed are, perhaps, sentimentalists. Call us that if you wish, but we gave our blood and sweat, and we deserve to be heard.

Once, we had communication between city and country and contact with the natural world around us. Today, this is being lost. With Standard of Living we are losing civilization. With Public Relations we are losing the pillars of that civilization – good manners, truth and sincerity.

That man cannot call himself civilized who, having by chemical sprays destroyed or banished from his garden the birds and animals, replaces them with pink flamingos in plywood – vulgar in concept, shoddy in construction and inartistic in appearance.

Say this is inevitable; say that time marches on and that Progress must be served; say what you like – but do not tell me that this is good, desirable or civilized.

Is this our revenge for Eden?

For over sixty years we have in this country set our hearts on destruction. "Wild" Saskatchewan has gone forever. What we could not do with horses and boats we have accomplished with bulldozers and airplanes. The wilderness is gone. There is no sanctuary. Must all living creatures go too?

I cannot believe that the people of Canada are willing to live in constant conflict with nature, but if they are not they must act – and quickly. We shall have to realign ourselves. We shall have to decide whether we shall go on letting nature be exploited or whether we shall protect the wildlife for the real reasons – first, that native culture may be preserved; secondly, that future generations will not be robbed of irreplaceable aesthetic treasures; and lastly that we shall cease to pay only lip service to the concept of the sanctity of life. "The right to live" cannot, surely, be confined to a species which spends so much of its talent and income in devising means of inflicting horrible and violent death even upon its own members.

The world of nature is at least innocent of this.

I suggest that my fellow countrymen take this seriously and see to it that full and adequate protective measures be put into force.

The alternative is a short life and a not too merry one, for in the destruction of our ecological environment we destroy ourselves.

ROBERT DAVID SYMONS

R.D. Symons was born in Sussex, England in 1898 to a well-off and educated family. The wanderlust bug bit him early and he emigrated to Canada while still a teenager, joining the Canadian Army Infantry in 1915 and the Imperial Army Fusiliers in 1918. He worked as a cowboy, rancher, game warden, naturalist and lecturer before establishing a career as an artist and writer later in his life. His popular books – two of which became Book-of-the-Month Club selections – include *Many Trails, Hours and the Birds, The Broken Snare, Still the Wind Blows, Where the Wagon Led: One Man's Memories of the Cowboy's Life in the Old West, North by West* and *Stilton Seasons: From the Diary of a Countryman.* His paintings are represented in private and public collections, including the Glenbow Museum, Edmonton Art Gallery, Royal Saskatchewan Museum and Bank of Montreal.

Symons married twice and was the father of four children. During his lifetime, he received a number of honours, including the Conservation Award from the Saskatchewan Natural History Society and an LL.D. from the University of Saskatchewan. He died in 1973.